RUGBY SHORTS

Chris Rhys

Illustrations by David Arthur

GUINNESS PUBLISHING

Editor: Charles Richards
Design and Layout: Michael Morey

© Chris Rhys and Guinness Publishing Ltd, 1990

Published in Great Britain by Guinness Publishing Ltd,
33 London Road, Enfield, Middlesex

Typeset in Galliard
by Ace Filmsetting Ltd, Frome, Somerset
Printed and bound in Great Britain by The Bath Press, Bath

'Guinness' is a registered trade mark of Guinness Superlatives Ltd

British Library Cataloguing in Publication Data
Rhys, Chris, *1942–*
  Rugby shorts
  1. Rugby football
  I. Title
  796.33′3

  ISBN 0–85112–324–4

CHRIS RHYS would like to believe that he would have played 100 times for Wales if only the selectors had bothered to investigate the talent on show at Millfield School, St Luke's College, Exeter, and London Welsh. The problem is that the selectors WERE there! At school, to check on Gareth Edwards and J P R Williams; at St Luke's to see Jeff Young, Dickie Uzzell and company (even England came for Don Rutherford and Mike Davis) and at London Welsh in the 1970s to spy on just about everybody else in the side!

Moments from his own career – during which Taunton, Minehead and Somerset also benefited from the Rhys magic – that might have found a home in the columns of this book include playing on the wing for the victorious London Welsh side at the Kent Sevens, yet failing to score a try in the eight games, despite being selected as 'the runner in'; turning out in Hush Puppies for the entire first part of a season during a search for employment; and being part of a team at Minehead whose record was so bad that a 36–0 win in a friendly against a local village cricket team was included in club records to boost the season's tally. None of the cricketers had ever played the rugby game . . .

But if nothing else happened to plan, at least he knew exactly when to pack it all in. After going to watch an International XV at Imber Court, being told to play because Gerald Davies couldn't make it and scoring four tries in the second half from a total distance of 15 yards, he retired on the spot and on the way home threw his boots onto the Kingston by-pass.

Chris Rhys now works for ITV on *The Match* and the athletics circuit, does research for overseas rugby and quiz programmes, and researches documentaries. He has written 15 books, including *Rugby: The Records*, published by Guinness.

CONTENTS

IN THE BEGINNING . . .

The London into which the Rugby Football Union came into existence in 1871 was in the middle of vast improvements, but was still, in the main, more like the London that Dickens wrote about than the London we know today. Highgate was still a village, Richmond was a convenient spot for nice people to spend a day or two near the river, the Underground was full of sulphurous fumes, and the Victoria and Albert Embankment was a new phenomenon. Nash's Quadrant in Regent Street was well established, but Shaftesbury and Northumberland Avenues were yet to feature on the map. And no one walked alone through Drury Lane, Soho and the Seven Dials.

Public transport was still in its elementary stage – uncomfortable, uncertain and rickety – except for that unique vehicle, the hansom cab. The stage coaches had nearly all vanished, the well-to-do went to work in private conveyances, some even on horse-back. Only a much-favoured street like Pall Mall had gas lamps. The Pall Mall Restaurant – where Rugby Union was born – has now long since disappeared from its original site.

In 1871 the social atmosphere was more unsettled than people would care to admit. The Indian Mutiny had received short shrift, and although the Prussians were in Paris, no one cared very much. The Crimean War and public hangings were easily discussed.

Sport was in its infancy – horse racing was largely supported by the gentry and the riff-raff in strange but friendly conjunction, as was boxing. Polo had just reached Hurlingham, while athletics and football were University sports but never mentioned within earshot of a rower. One WG Grace was 23 years old.

Rugby, the domain of the Public schools and their Old Boys, was born into this uncertainty. But the only thing that mattered, of course, was that the time was ripe for the formation of the Rugby Football Union . . .

The Rugby Union's first seven matches were played at Kennington Oval. It was quite simply the only playing field suitable in all London where rugby could be played. The annual subscription to the Rugby Union was 5/- per club.

For the first Scotland v England international on 27 March 1871 the England players travelled up overnight, third class, and paid their own expenses, while many of the Scotland team played in long cricket whites tucked into their socks. Scotland's winning try was adjudged by H H Almond, headmaster of Loretto, who commented, 'I decided against the side making the most noise. Teams that do that are probably in the wrong.'

The entrance charges for the first England match at the Oval, against Scotland in 1872, were: persons on foot 1/-; carriages 5/-; drags and omnibuses 10/-.

Redruth RFC used the Redruth Brewery Ground in 1874. The pitch included a huge stone post in the middle and the footpath took the main traffic of those days from Redruth to neighbouring Cambourne.

Matches sometimes took all afternoon.

RMA Woolwich withdrew their offer of a Challenge Cup for clubs after rejection by special RFU sub-committee. (*RFU Report 1875–6*)

Idea of national Challenge Cup raised again but met with little approval. Kent introduced a Cup competition to prevent game from dying out in parts of the county. (*RFU Report 1880–1*)

The 1877 West Wales Challenge Cup final between Cardiff and Llanelly (as it was then spelt) had to be abandoned because the crowd stole the ball.

In 1884–5 Swansea RFC accused Cardiff RFC: 'The figures of Cardiff RFC show that £364 2s 3d was taken at the gate alone. We believe that the club is paying players' railway fares and hotel expenses, if not more.'

On 1 March 1884, England beat Scotland by one goal to one try. Scotland did not accept the result until 1886 and then only on condition that the Rugby Union formed an International Board to settle future disputes.

In 1887 Ireland beat England for the first time. The treasurer's report read, 'There is a reluctance to play outside Ireland. Matches tend to be expensive. An escapade in a waxworks cost us £50, whilst a ceremony known as Highland Honours – viz: smashing champagne glasses and bottles against a wall of a dining room covered with mirrors – has set us back another £80.'

'Scotland are very rough, and there is scarcely an Ireland v Scotland match in which two or three Irishmen have not been carried from the field.'

J J McCarthy: *The Rugby Game* 1892

The link between rugby and its social backgrounds had early roots. *The Cambrian* of 24 March 1893 quoted a speech by a Mr Michael Craven, who said, 'Rugby football was the fascination of the devil and the twin sister of the drinking system, and without the latter it would have a job to succeed.' There were frequent agreements from the audience.

One of the new rules for 1897 stated that 'an injured player, who has retired from the game and is standing on the touch line, can tackle a player on the pitch provided that he is not offside'.

The first England v New Zealand match took place in 1905–6 at the Crystal Palace. New Zealand won by five tries (15 points) to nil. The crowd was 45 000 and the takings were £1 039 13s 11d.

East Midlands were beaten 14–5 by the 1912 Springboks at Franklin Gardens, Northampton, but had developed an unusual plan for keeping the score to reasonable proportions. No sooner was the ball put in to the scrum, than on the call 'scatter' the entire pack fled from the scrum, leaving the Springboks in confusion and disarray.

On the same 1912 tour, London evolved another method. They would allow themselves to be pushed away from the line of scrummage on 'at least eight occasions' per scrum. This frustration did much to enable London to secure a shock win 10–8.

'What do you mean by coming off the field smiling? You lost!'

The art of captaincy from TW Gubb, captain of Blackheath: 'What are our young men coming to, and of what material are they made, that, when they have committed some unpardonable offence, they are not to be handed their gruel in time-honoured fashion? I often used the phrase, "Damned fool". I am forced to take this ferocious view of the duties of captain because I detect a waning virility in the game . . . I shall resign at the end of the season, as I am fed up with puling infants.'

Jubilee Dinner of Edinburgh Academicals, 20 March 1908, from Sir J H A McDonald: 'Very few have seen a proper scrum. Had they ever seen a haystack that had been put up when the hay was wet, and the smoke and steam was rising from it? That

was just like a scrum in those days, and just about as motionless.'

By the 1920s the game had moved on a great deal. Or had it? The leading book of the era, *Rugby Football Today*, was written by E H D Sewell. Some of the contents have a familiar ring even today . . .

'If coaches want to do a good job–as they seem to have nothing else to do–they should work out some new ways over the try line, and thus help to switch this game of ours off the road towards Monotony upon which it is certainly staggering today.'

'Why, many forwards in these modern days do not even watch the ball!'

'Good kicking is an asset in any position, but there is a great tendency to overdo it by fly-halves. A fly-half is there solely to open up the game, not to kick to touch.'

'I have never been a strong believer in the 3–2–3 formation in the scrum. The 3–3–2 method is the best every time. Ask those New Zealanders.'

'The parrot cry of "inside" will mar, and probably already has marred, more wings than it will make, or has ever made. Thus our wings are seldom trained to go all out for the corner.'

'The chief qualification for a full back is what phrenologists call the bump of locality. Without this precious bump of locality a full-back will seldom be in the right place to catch the ball.'

'Noise does not connote good leadership.'

'Anybody who can rid Rugby football of that hyphenated nuisance, the wing-forward, will do this game a power of good. The modern scrummage consists of five forwards and three hybrids–obstructors who don't know what they are doing, a perpetual nuisance and menace

to everyone. The game is becoming a travesty of what is is intended to be.'

'The best leadership of all is "Silent Example" – like the 1906 Springbok Paul Roos, who only opened his mouth to eat.'

From Dr R Cove Smith: 'They all talk about Eric Liddell, but he has no speed and lacks the required class.' (Liddell went on to win the gold medal in the 400 metres at the 1924 Olympics – later he was the subject of the film *Chariots of Fire*)

'A referee can make or mar a match, and a noisy referee always mars.'

London Referees Dinner, 1928

'It is at least debatable whether our game has derived any real benefit from the numbering of players. Players exist who are not above keeping an eye on the Press box in order to be noticed. Numbering players tends to increase this evil.'

A more optimistic view came from CCHoyer Miller in his *50 Years of Rosslyn Park*, published in 1929: 'The three greatest civilizing influences since the Christian era, are to be found in the work of the Salvation Army, secondly the institution of the Boy Scouts, and thirdly in the spread of outdoor games, especially Rugby football. My belief is that the importance of Rugby football in the formation both of individual and national character is becoming increasingly profound.'

Clubs in full control of their grounds are advised not to allow greyhound racing. (*RFU Report 1927*)

Rugby by floodlight for gate money prohibited as being not in the best interests of the game. (*RFU Report 1932*)

In 1946, Ilkley Rugby Club were refused permission by the RFU to lend their ground to the New Zealand Rugby League touring team in return for a fee to help them modernise their ground. A resolution to the contrary was heavily defeated.

The first programme at a Rugby Union international at Twickenham was for the England v South Africa match in 1951–2. The cost was 1/-. For the following international v France the signature of the RFU secretary appeared on the cover to defeat 'pirate' programmes.

The actual purchase price of Twickenham in 1907 was £5 572 12s 6d – the ground was originally a cabbage patch, with vegetables, fruit trees and mushrooms grown on the site.

Twickenham's weather vane, which took the place of the old clock tower on the South Terrace in 1950 was designed by a Mr Kenneth Dalgleish.

THE WIDE WORLD
OF RUGBY

ODD ORIGINS

Many countries have been lucky enough to receive constructive organization and coaching advice from the old British colonial countries and France and its dependencies. Others though were not so fortunate . . .

Czechoslovakia were indebted to Andrej Sekora, a writer of children's books, who went to Paris, bought a book of rules, translated them, and formed a club.

Holland owe much to Pim Mulder who came back from London with a rugby ball in 1879. Wherever Mulder went with his ball, a game broke out.

Fijian players never wore boots until expressly told to do so for the visit of the New Zealand Maoris in 1938. Most had had enough of 'Western culture' by half-time.

Yugoslavia had a problem with the rules. In 1957 they formed their own league, and when France sent a representative side there in 1961, the Yugoslavs were found to be playing Rugby League. Whether they were ignorant of the fact that the League code is professional or not is unclear, but in 1964 the Yugoslavs opted for the 15-a-side game.

The Barbarians were a famous side long before 1948, but in that year they played a touring team in the now traditional close-of-tour game for the first time. The touring Australians were believed to be so financially embarrassed that another game had to be arranged to fund the journey home – so they played the Barbarians.

Some of the emerging clubs and nations have had difficulties coming to terms with the local terrain in their efforts to construct viable playing surfaces . . .

Bahrain play on sandy pitches, as indeed are most playing fields in the Gulf States. Their best pitch is at Muharraq, by the side of the main runway of Bahrain International Airport.

Barbados had a pitch which was hewn out of the tangled centre of a race-track. The first club was called the Barbados Night Club.

Gibraltar have no grass on their only pitch, so that a form of rugby with local rules called Tag Rugby has to be played.

Holland and **Portugal** both play a version of beach rugby. The Dutch League was continued on the beaches in 1978–9 when foul weather threatened disruption of fixtures. In Portugal beach rugby, especially for the young, is a feature of the development policy within the country and has been for many years.

Indonesia have a pitch in the jungle at Kalimantan, and another on the steepest hillside imaginable at a tea plantation.

Japan have a problem with space. One of their international pitches, at Yokohama, doubles as a women's hockey pitch, a golf driving-range and a soccer pitch.

The Seychelles have a ground that was created out of a landslide after a cyclone.

Western Samoa staged their first international against Fiji at Apia in 1924. The game kicked of at 7am so that the local players could get to work. The pitch had a large tree on the halfway line.

Several other apparently genuine grounds would test the belief of sceptics . . .

League matches in **Asian** countries where the local naval team has been invited to play have taken place on the decks of ships.

Fijian provincial pitches invariably have concrete all-weather cricket squares in the centre.

Amman RFC and teams from construction companies regularly play on the floor of the **Dead Sea**. The pitch, made out of soft sand, lies 1 286ft (385m) below sea level, and a scroll is given to those who have been invited to play at the venue.

The Soviet League contains at least three teams from **Siberia**, CSKA Novosibersk, Polytechnic Krasnoyarsk, and CSKA Bakal. The Soviet season runs from April through to November, but the start and finish of the season often include matches in which weather conditions are totally

unreasonable. So much so that a team from Leningrad filled in a form in 1984 saying they had lost 6–0 in Krasnoyarsk in a League match, when they had not been within a thousand miles of the place!

SUPERLATIVE LOCATIONS

The highest international rugby ground is Ellis Park in Johannesburg, South Africa which is 5 940ft (1 810m) above sea level. The Wanderers ground in the same city is 200ft (61m) higher, but internationals have not been played there for some time.

With many major international grounds being situated in cities at sea level, there can be no accurate assessment of the lowest international grounds. However, it is worth recording the fact that the Dutch National Stadium in Hilversum, which is used for Holland's home FIRA championship matches, is, like the country itself, below sea level.

The most northerly international rugby ground is Murrayfield, in Edinburgh,

Scotland, which is 55.57°N. However, the Soviet Union, who play in Group A of the FIRA championship, have on several occasions used their ground at Leningrad for international matches. Leningrad is at 59.55°N.

The most southerly major rugby ground is Rugby Park in Invercargill, New Zealand which is 46.24°S. Southland RU, the hosts at Invercargill, have played most major international touring teams, but have yet to host a full international. International rugby has often been staged in Dunedin, New Zealand, at Carisbrook Park. One international has also been staged at Tahuna Park in the same city.

WEATHER REPORTS

A temperature of 33°C was reported during the international between South Africa and the British Isles at Port Elizabeth in 1938. Most of the players were so tired after the match that they went straight to bed. The match has become known as 'The Tropical Test'. South Africa won 19–3 but it is reported that the British Isles players, coping admirably, were well on top in the closing stages of the match.

Extremes of cold, as with heat, are not recorded, but several French teams have returned from Bucharest and Moscow stating that FIRA championship matches have been played on frozen turf and snow at a ground temperature of −15°C. The 1988 match in Bucharest between Romania and France, won by France 16–12, was a particularly cold exercise – the temperature was −18°C!

On 21 February 1885, at Ormeau, Belfast, a storm waterlogged the pitch during an Ireland v Scotland international. With a fierce gale and snow making play impossible, the match was called off 25 minutes into the first half, with Scotland leading by a try to nil. The match was later replayed in Edinburgh with the Scots winning by a goal and two tries to nil on 7 March 1885 at Raeburn Place.

COLOUR CO-ORDINATED

NEW ZEALAND

The New Zealand Rugby Union was formed in 1892, and for the first match under their jurisdiction the team were kitted out in a black jersey, white fern, and white shorts for the match against New South Wales in 1894. When New Zealand played the same opponents in 1901 however, photos from the game show the players wearing black shorts.

When the first New Zealand team went on tour to New South Wales in 1884, they wore dark blue jersies with a gold fern, but this was before the NZRFU was founded.

SOUTH AFRICA

Barry Heatlie was South Africa's captain for their first ever international victory, 5–0 against the British Isles in 1896. On that occasion Heatlie brought the green shirts of his own club, Old Diocesan Old Boys RFC of Cape Town. Flushed with their success, the South Africans promptly dropped Heatlie, and did not recall him until the third Test of the next British tour. By this time though, Heatlie's club side had been disbanded. However, the outfitters still had supplies of the club kit in stock. Heatlie, again made captain, was asked to repossess the kit, largely for good luck purposes. South Africa took the field in green shirts, white collars and black shorts – with red socks borrowed from the Villagers RFC, also of Cape Town. The British Isles team won 9–3 at Kimberley. On 12 September 1906, three years to the day after the Kimberley Test, the South African Rugby Board settled on the colours because they had been worn for their first two major wins. In 1937, the shorts were changed

to white, the collars to old gold and the socks to green.

AUSTRALIA

Australia's present colours of gold shirts and green shorts were first used on their 1961 tour to South Africa where they lost both Tests handsomely. Despite this, the Wallabies stuck to the colours to avoid clashes with South Africa's more established colours (see above) of green shirts and gold collars.

ALL BLACKS AND OTHER NICKNAMES

The New Zealand tourists to Britain in 1905–6 were given the name 'Blacks' by the *Daily Mail* before the match with Northampton on 28 September 1905. The phrase '**All Blacks**' appeared in the columns of the same newspaper on 12 October 1905 following the 63–0 demolition of Hartlepool clubs on the previous day. Ironically the score still remains the highest by the 'All Blacks' on any tour to the British Isles.

A year after the New Zealand All Blacks' visit, South Africa made their first visit to the British

Isles. Before the first training session, the media asked whether the team had a nickname. Paul Roos, the tour captain, said that the unanimous choice of himself, the team, and tour manager JC Carden was that it be **De Springbokken** or **Springboks**.

The first Australian tour to Britain was in 1908–9 to England and Wales. The team then had a live snake mascot called Bertie but declined to be called Berties. The players chose the name **Wallabies** by a short head from 'The Wolves'.

On the 1965 tour to South Africa, the Argentinians played Rhodesia (now Zimbabwe) in Salisbury (now Harare). The crest on their jerseys depicted a jaguar, but local journalists mistook the jaguar for a puma. The name **Pumas**, though clearly wrong, stuck; Rhodesia won 17–12.

The first British tour officially sanctioned by the four Home Unions was to Australia and New Zealand in 1930. Prior to that, tours and selections were by invitation. The motif chosen for the tour was a lion and the team is known as the **British Lions**, but use the name British Isles for international matches only.

CUPS GONGS & SHIELDS

The **Bledisloe Cup** is played annually between Australia and New Zealand. The Cup was donated by the Governor General of New Zealand, Lord Bledisloe, in 1931.

The **Currie Cup**, the premier trophy in South Africa, was presented by Sir Donald Currie, the founder of the shipping line, to WE MacLagan, the captain of the first British Isles tourists to the country in 1891, for him to donate to the team which had performed best against them. Griqualand West were the team selected to hold the Cup; they, in turn, presented the Cup to the South African Rugby Board, who, in turn presented it as a trophy for the winners of the Inter Union championship.

The **Ranfurly Shield** is the premier domestic trophy in New Zealand. The Shield was presented by Lord Ranfurly, Governor of New Zealand, in 1902 to be contested by all Unions affiliated to the NZRU. Auckland were the first winners on merit, but since then, each holder has had to resist challenges from other Unions in order to retain it.

The **Calcutta Cup** has been contested by England and Scotland since 1878. The previous year, the Calcutta RFC in India had been disbanded due to lack of suitable opposition; club funds were used to provide a trophy for an annual competition between England and Scotland. The trophy, made out of actual rupees withdrawn from the bank, took the form of a tapered Cup, with three snake handles and a model elephant as the lid piece. The inscription on the Calcutta Cup reads:

THE CALCUTTA CUP
PRESENTED TO THE RUGBY
FOOTBALL UNION
BY THE CALCUTTA FOOTBALL
CLUB AS AN INTERNATIONAL
CHALLENGE TROPHY
TO BE PLAYED FOR ANNUALLY BY
ENGLAND AND SCOTLAND
1878

It is generally accepted that the **International Championship** began in 1882–3, although the four Home Nations had played each other periodically since the first international match between Scotland and England at Raeburn Place, Edinburgh on Monday 20 March 1871. In 1882–3 the four Home Nations played each other on a round robin basis for the first time, though Ireland and Wales did not meet. France joined in 1909–10.

The **FIRA Championship**, of the Federation Internationale de Rugby Amateur, which is a league containing such countries as France, Romania, the Soviet Union, Italy and Spain, was first contested in 1973–4 on a Championship basis. There is now an 'A' Group, two regional 'B' Groups and a 'C' Group of emerging European and North African rugby-playing countries.

The **Russell Cargill Memorial Cup** is awarded to the winners of the Middlesex Sevens.

The **Lloyd Lewis Memorial Cup** is awarded to the man of the match in the Welsh Cup final. Lloyd Lewis was the rugby correspondent of the *News of the World* who died in the Paris air disaster of 1974, when returning from the France v England match at the Parc des Princes.

The **Webb Ellis Trophy** is the award for the winners of rugby's World Cup, first contested in 1987 and won by New Zealand.

The **Mobbs Memorial Match** is played annually between the East Midlands and the Barbarians at Northampton. It commemorates the fine Northampton and England three-quarter Edgar Mobbs, who was killed in action during the First World War, in 1917.

The **English Cup** was sponsored by **John Player** from its inception in 1971–2 until 1988–9, when it became known as the **Pilkington Cup**.

The **Lion Cup** has been contested since 1983 in South Africa and is the country's major knock-out tournament. The **Toyota Cup** is the country's major domestic club competition. Begun in 1975, it is a knock-out tournament held over the Easter weekend between the champion clubs of the major provinces.

The **National Championship** in New Zealand was started in 1975. Run on a League basis, it has three divisions and is open to all the provinces. It acts as a complement to the challenge for the Ranfurly Shield.

The **French Club Championship** was first played in 1892. The final was refereed by the founder of the modern Olympic movement, Baron Pierre de Coubertin.

Domestic rugby in Australia is centred around the Premiership finals for clubs at Brisbane and Sydney. New South Wales and Queensland have been meeting at state level since 1884.

OLYMPIC RUGBY

Just about the most often asked quiz question is the one concerning the current Olympic rugby champions. Those who have heard the question know the answer, those who have not can spend all evening failing to come up with the right answer. The USA are the reigning Olympic champions of an event played at four Olympics, where the standard has varied between excellent and downright ridiculous!

The 1900 Games were staged in Paris, and were the brainchild of Pierre de Coubertin, the founder of the modern Olympic movement and a rugby fanatic. He played the game, and refereed the first French championship final. Rugby was a must as an Olympic sport as far as he was concerned.

Rugby was a major sport at the 1900 games, though only three countries took part. Other Olympic sports included golf, cricket, and an obstacle race on the Seine! France won gold, having beaten Britain (alias Moseley Wanderers) 27–7 and Germany (alias FSV Frankfurt) 27–17. The Germany v Britain match never took place, so the lesser medals were decided on the scores in the matches against France. Germany took silver, Britain bronze. Any one not recognizing the teams immediately would have been given a large clue – eight of the French team wore berets!

In 1908, London hosted the games and just one match was played, at the White City. The Australians, who were on their first tour to Britain, beat Cornwall, the champion English county who were representing Britain, by 32–3. It was the Australians' ninth match of the tour, their only loss before the Olympic final being against Llanelly, a result which prompted the locals to insert 'Who beat the Wallabies' into their song, 'Sospan Fach'.

The 1920 Games took place at Antwerp and who won gold depends on what side's version is read! That the USA played France is about the only common factor to the entire story! David Wallechinsky's book on the history of the Olympics, which has fast become an Olympic bible, states that the USA beat France 8–0 on 20 May. The French story is totally different. Henri Garcia's widely respected *Encyclopedia of Rugby* claims a French gold medal on 10 October! France won 14–5 against a team, predominantly from Stanford University, who arrived in Antwerp expecting to play American football; a call was sent to Baron de Coubertin's French office asking for a match in Paris. Both reports are well chronicled and what is apparent is that there were several thousand servicemen still in Europe after the First World War. The crux of the problem is that no official Olympic Report exists for Antwerp, the only Olympics which are impossible to research. But most sports historians tend to award the gold medal to the USA.

In 1924, Romania, France and the USA entered the rugby event in Paris. The Americans were again largely drawn from Stanford University, as there was no official US Rugby Union and the players were enthusiasts who rallied to the call to 'defend' their 1920 title. The recruits went by car through the USA, by boat to the United Kingdom, played three games in England, and then went across the channel to France. Both France and the USA beat Romania easily before what proved to be the last Olympic final took place at Colombes Stadium on 18 May 1924. The USA shocked a 40 000 crowd by winning 17–3, five tries to one against the 20–1 on favourites. So upset were the French that they booed the US anthem, and Gideon Nelson never received his medal. He was stunned by a blow from an irate Frenchwoman's umbrella.

OLYMPIC RESULTS

1900
France 27 Germany 17
France 27 Great Britain 7

1908
Australia 32 Great Britain 3

1920
Either USA 8 France 0
or France 14 USA 5

1924
France 59 Romania 3
USA 37 Romania 0
USA 17 France 3

There was no rugby at the 1904 Olympics in St Louis due mainly to travel difficulties, nor in 1896 (Athens) or 1912 (Stockholm) due to lack of rugby knowledge in the host country.

GOLD MEDALLISTS

Of the gold medallists from the four Olympic finals, two are particularly worthy of mention . . .

Daniel Carroll is the only player to have won gold medals in Rugby Union for two countries – for Australia in 1908 and for the USA in 1920*. Born on 17 November 1889, he played for St George's and New South Wales. He was a member of the 1908–9 Australian squad which toured Britain, playing in the international against Wales. He was a right winger, and 'the quickest member of the team'. In 1912 he was chosen to tour the USA and won his second and final cap. Carroll remained in the United States and became player-coach at Stanford University, California. With the US team for the 1920 Games based around the Stanford side, Carroll gained his second gold twelve years after his first success. He died in 1957, aged 68.

Morris Kirksey won gold medals in two different sports at the 1920 Olympics. On 9 May he won gold in the rugby final* along with his fellow Stanford University team mates. On 16 August, he gained the silver medal in the 100 metres in 10.8 seconds, the same time as the winner Charlie Paddock. On 22 August he ran the anchor leg in the USA 4 × 100 metres relay team, which not only won the gold medal in 42.2 seconds, but beat by a tenth of a second the existing world record set by Germany.

* There is still dispute as to which 1920 match counted for the gold medal (*see page 25*).

NAME THAT TEAM

ENGLAND

9 Smith
9 Taylor
8 Scott
8 Wilson
7 Roberts
7 Williams
7 Wright

SCOTLAND

12 Smith
11 Brown
11 Robertson
10 McDonald
(incl. Macdonald)
10 Wilson

IRELAND

11 Brown
(incl. 4 Browne)
8 Kennedy
7 Moore
6 O'Connor
6 Ross
6 Hewitt
6 Murphy

WALES

56 Jones
52 Davies
42 Evans
41 Williams
32 Thomas
21 Morgan
18 Rees
16 Lewis

FRANCE

4 Fabre
4 Martin
3 Camberabero
3 Carrère
3 Du Pont
3 Haget
3 Lacaze
3 Lasserre
3 Laurent

SOUTH AFRICA

10 Morkel
9 Du Plessis
6 Van Der Merwe
5 Botha
5 De Villiers
5 Du Toit
5 Louw
5 Smith
5 Van Zyl

NEW ZEALAND

8 Smith
7 Wilson
6 Taylor
6 Clarke
(incl. 2 Clark)
4 Harvey
4 McGregor
4 Oliver
4 Reid
4 Stewart
4 White

AUSTRALIA

7 McLean
7 White
6 Davis
5 Smith
5 Thompson
4 Brown
4 Miller
4 Richards
4 Williams

INTERNATIONALS WITH BRITISH PLACE NAMES

ENGLAND

Ashby, RC
Barnes, S
Bedford, H
Bedford, LL
Bolton, CA
Bolton, R
Bolton, WN
Buckingham, RA
Burton, GW
Burton, HC
Burton, MA
Conway, GS
Hanley, J
Hastings, GWD
Hyde, JP

Kendall, PD
Kingston, P
Newbold, CJ
Oldham, WL
Pickering, RDA
Poole, FO
Poole, RW
Preston, NJ
Rotherham, A
Stafford, RC
Stafford, WHF
Stirling, RV
Wakefield, WW
Wells, CM

REST OF THE WORLD

Barnes, IA (Scotland)
Barnes, RJ (Ireland)
Barry, EF (New Zealand)
Barry, J (South Africa)
Barry, MJ (Australia)
Bedford, TP (South Africa)
Bolton, WH (Scotland)
Buxton, JB (New Zealand)
Glasgow, RJC (Scotland)
Glasgow, FT (New Zealand)
Hamilton, AS (Scotland)
Hamilton, HM (Scotland)
Hamilton, BG (Australia)
Hamilton, F (South Africa)
Hamilton, DC (New Zealand)
Hamilton, AJ (Ireland)
Hamilton, RL (Ireland)
Hamilton, RW (Ireland)
Hamilton, WJ (Ireland)
Hastings, AG (Scotland)
Hastings, S (Scotland)
Lambourn, A (New Zealand)
Leeds, AJ (Australia)
Manchester JE (New Zealand)
Mansfield, BW (Australia)
Melrose JC (Australia)
Moffat, J (Ireland)
Morley, JC (Wales)
Roxburgh, JR (Australia)
Sutton, S (Wales)
Windsor, RW (Wales)
Windsor, JG (Australia)

Badger, O (Wales)
Bull, AG (England)
Camel, A (France)
Camel, F (France)
Coote, PB (Ireland)
Crowe, JF (Ireland)
Crowe, L (Ireland)
Crowe, MP (Ireland)
Crowe, PM (Ireland)
Crowe, PJ (Australia)
McCrow, JWS (Scotland)
Drake-Lee, NJ (England)
Finch, RT (England)
Finch, E (Wales)
Fox, FH (England)
Fox, J (Scotland)
Fox, GJ (New Zealand)
Fox, OG (Australia)
Gibbons, E de C (Australia)
Hare, WH (England)
Heron, G (Scotland)
Heron, AG (Ireland)
Heron, J (Ireland)
Heron, JW (Ireland)
Lyon, A (England)
Lyon, GHD'o (England)
Mackrell, WHC (New Zealand)
Peacock, H (Wales)
Pike, TO (Ireland)
Pike, VJ (Ireland)
Pike, WW (Ireland)
Robbins, GL (England)
Robbins, PGD (England)
Robins, JD (Wales)
Robins, RJ (Wales)
Salmon, JLB (England/New
   Zealand)
Sole, DMB (Scotland)
Sparrow, W (Ireland)
Stagg, PK (Scotland)
Swan, JS (Scotland)
Swan, MW (Scotland)
Swift, AH (England)
Wolfe, EJ (Ireland)
Wolfe, TN (New Zealand)

ENGLAND

Archer, H
Baker, DGS
Baker, EM
Baker, HC
Bishop, CC
Brewer, J
Butcher, CJS
Butcher, WV
Butler, AG
Carpenter, AD
Clark, CWH
Clarke, AJ
Clarke, SJS
Cook, JG
Cook, PW
Cooke, DA
Cooke, DH
Cooke, P
Cooper, JG
Cooper, MJ
Cowman, AR
Fidler, JH
Fletcher, NC
Fletcher, T
Fletcher, WRB
Gardner, ER
Gardner, HP
Parsons, EI
Parsons, MJ
Plummer, KC
Sheppard, A
Sherriff, GA
Tanner, CC
Taylor, AS
Taylor, EW
Taylor, F
Taylor, FM
Taylor, HH
Taylor, JT
Taylor, PJ
Taylor, RB
Taylor, WJ

Allison, DF (England)
Allison, JB (Ireland)
Carroll, C (Ireland)
Carroll, R (Ireland)
Carroll, DB (Australia)
Carroll, JC (Australia)
Carroll, JH (Australia)
Clare, J (Wales)
Dee, JM (England)
Ella, GA (Australia)
Ella, GJ (Australia)
Ella, MG (Australia)
Elsey, WJ (Wales)
Fay, G (Australia)
Francis, JAJ (South Africa)
Francis, E (Australia)
Francis, TES (England)
Francis, DG (Wales)
Gale, NR (Wales)
Gay, DJ (England)
Gill, AD (Scotland)
Grace, TO (Ireland)
Gracie, AL (Scotland)
Hannah, RSM (Scotland)
Hazell, DSG (England)
Hillary, MF (Ireland)
Joyce, JE (Australia)
Kay, AR (Australia)
Leslie, AR (New Zealand)
Leslie, DG (Scotland)
Lindsay, RTG (Australia)
Lindsay, AB (Scotland)
Lindsay, GC (Scotland)
Lindsay, DF (New Zealand)
Lindsay, H (Ireland)
Lorraine, HDB (Scotland)
Madge, RJP (England)
Martine, R (France)
Maud, P (England)
Penny, SH (England)
Penny, WJ (England)
Rose, WHM (England)
Rose, HA (Australia)
Rose, DM (Scotland)
Tillie, CR (Ireland)
Vivyan, EJ (England)

Barley, B (England)
Beer, IDS (England)
Berry, CW (Scotland)
Berry, H (England)
Berry, J (England)
Berry, JTW (England)
Burger, MB (South Africa)
Burger, SWP (South Africa)
Burger, WAG (South Africa)
Cordial, IF (Scotland)
Currey, FI (England)
Currie, C (South Africa)
Currie, EW (Australia)
Currie, CJ (New Zealand)
Currie, JD (England)
Currie, LR (Scotland)
Lemon, A (Wales)
Mackrell, WHC (New Zealand)
Pike, TO (Ireland)
Pike, VJ (Ireland)
Pike, WW (Ireland)
Salmon, JLB (New Zealand/
  England)
Sherry, BF (Ireland)
Sherry, MJA (Ireland)
Sole, DMB (Scotland)
Stout, FM (England)
Stout, PW (England)
Sweet, JB (Scotland)
Waters, DR (Wales)
Waters, FH (Scotland)
Waters, JA (Scotland)
Waters, JB (Scotland)

Ash, WH (Ireland)
Barley, B (England)
Barnes, S (England)
Barnes, IA (Scotland)

31

Barnes, RJ (Ireland)
Berry, H (England)
Berry, J (England)
Berry, JT (England)
Berry, W (England)
Birch, J (Wales)
Brook, PWP (England)
Brooke, TJ (England)
Budd, A (England)
Budd, TA (New Zealand)
Bush, RJ (New Zealand)
Bush, WK (New Zealand)
Bush, JA (England)
Bush, PF (Wales)
Cave, JW (England)
Cave, WTC (England)
Dyke, JCM (Wales)
Dyke, LM (Wales)
Dykes, AS (Scotland)
Dykes, JC (Scotland)
Dykes, JM (Scotland)
Farmer, EH (Australia)
Fell, AN (Scotland)
Field, E (England)
Forrest, JW (England)
Forrest, R (England)
Forrest, JE (Scotland)
Forrest, JGS (Scotland)
Forrest, WT (Scotland)
Forrest, AJ (Ireland)
Forrest, EG (Ireland)
Forrest, H (Ireland)

Glen, WS (Scotland)
Glenn, WS (New Zealand)
Hay, BH (Scotland)
Heath, AH (England)
Hill, SF (New Zealand)
Hill, CCP (Scotland)
Hill, RA (South Africa)
Hill, AF (Wales)
Hill, BA (England)

Hill, RJ (England)
Marsh, H (England)
Marsh, J (England)
Marsh, J (Scotland)
Meadows, JEC (Australia)
Meadows, RW (Australia)
Moss, F (England)
Moss, C (South Africa)
Poole, FO (England)
Poole, RW (England)
Rowan, NA (Scotland)

Shepherd, DJ (Australia)
Sheppard, A (England)
Stone, A (Australia)
Stone, CG (Australia)
Stone, JM (Australia)
Stone, F le S (England)
Stone, AM (New Zealand)
Stone, P (Wales)
Twigge, RJ (South Africa)
Warren, JR (Scotland)
Warren, RC (Scotland)
Warren, JP (Ireland)
Warren, RG (Ireland)
Wells, BG (Australia)
Wells, CM (England)
Wells, J (New Zealand)
Wells, GT (Wales)
Wells, HG (Ireland)
Wood, F (Australia)
Wood, RN (Australia)
Wood, GH (Ireland)
Wood, BGM (Ireland)
Wood, ME (New Zealand)
Wood, A (Scotland)
Wood, G (Scotland)
Wood, A (England)
Wood, AE (England)
Wood, GW (England)
Wood, R (England)
Wood, RD (England)

ENGLAND	Club	First cap
LE Barrington-Ward	Edinburgh Univ	1910
E Bonham-Carter	Oxford Univ	1891
B Braithwaite-Exley	Headingley	1949
R Cove-Smith	O.M.T.	1921
N J Drake-Lee	Cambridge Univ, Leicester	1963
E A Hamilton-Hill	Harlequins	1936
R H Hamilton-Wickes	Cambridge Univ	1924
G W Gordon-Smith	Blackheath	1900
P Horrocks-Taylor	Leicester, Middlesbrough	1958
Mac G K Kendall-Carpenter	Oxford Univ, Bath	1949
F A Leslie-Jones	Richmond	1895
E Maxwell-Hyslop	Oxford Univ	1922
Q Newton-Thompson	Oxford Univ	1947
H G Owen-Smith	St Mary's Hospital	1934
R W Poulton-Palmer	Harlequins	1909
G C Rittson-Thomas	Oxford Univ	1951
C F Stanger-Leathes	Northern	1905
N C Starmer-Smith	Harlequins	1969
M R Steele-Bodger	Cambridge Univ	1947
D Turquand-Young	Richmond	1928
A Vaughan-Jones	Army	1932
P B R W William-Powlett	Royal Navy	1922

SCOTLAND		
D R Bedell-Sivright	Cambridge Univ	1900
V Bedell-Sivright	Cambridge Univ	1902
H Bruce-Lockhart	London Scottish	1913
L Bruce-Lockhart	London Scottish	1948
R B Bruce-Lockhart	London Scottish	1937
R E Campbell-Lamerton	London Scottish	1986
M J Campbell-Lamerton	Halifax, Army, L Scottish	1967
A Clunies-Ross	St Andrews Univ	1871
D Crichton-Millar	Gloucester	1931
A R Don-Wauchope	Fettesian-Lorretonians	1881
P H Don-Wauchope	Fettesian-Lorretonians	1885
D S Gilbert-Smith	London Scottish	1952
R Hay-Gordon	Edinburgh Acads	1885
G C Hoyer-Millar	Oxford Univ	1953
R H Lindsay-Watson	Hawick	1909
E G Loudon-Shand	Oxford Univ	1913
H W Renny-Taylour	Royal Engineers	1872

IRELAND

S E F Blake-Knox	NIFC	1976
T R Johnson-Smyth	Lansdowne	1882
R H Massey-Westropp	Limerick & Monkstown	1886
J Murphy-O'Connor	Bective Rangers	1954
P E O'Brien-Butler	Monkstown	1897

WALES

J Conway-Rees	Llanelli	1892
T E Jones-Davies	London Welsh	1930
D Marsden-Jones	Cardiff	1921
T J Pryce-Jenkins	London Welsh	1888
G R Rees-Jones	Oxford Univ & London Welsh	1934
W Rice-Evans	Swansea	1890
D N Roycn-Jones	Cambridge Univ	1925
J Strand-Jones	Llanelli	1902
R B Sweet-Escott	Cardiff	1891
H Williams-Jones	South Wales Police	1989

FRANCE

R Berges-Cau	Lourdes	1976
J Chaban-Delmas	CASG Paris	1945
M-F Lubin-Lebrere	Toulouse	1914
J Prin-Clary	Brive	1945
M Tucoo-Chaalat	Paris Univ Club	1940

NEW ZEALAND

| M Brooke-Cowden | Auckland | 1986 |
| G A H Bullock-Douglas | Wanganui | 1932 |

AUSTRALIA

| N C Farr-Jones | New South Wales | 1984 |
| M Massey-Westrop | New South Wales | 1914 |

WERE THEY REALLY WELSHMEN?

These all played for Wales, but you wouldn't think so by their name:

Britton, GR
Cornish, FH
Cornish, RA
Darbishire, G
Wiltshire, ML

... WERE THESE IRISH?

English, MAF
Holland, JJ
Scott, D
Scott, RD
Spain, AW

... AND WERE THESE PLAYERS SCOTTISH?

France, C
French, J
Ireland, JCH
Turk, AS
Welsh, R
Welsh, R
Welsh, FWB
Welsh, WH

GREAT RUGBY FAMILIES

Several brothers have played rugby in the same national teams; fathers and sons have played international rugby; and several generations of families have all played at the highest level. But some of the more unusual family ties have been . . .

The only instances of three brothers playing in the same team at international level are those of **Freddie, Dick and John Luyt** of South Africa. On the 1912–13 tour to Britain they played against Scotland (won 16–0), Wales (won 3–0) and England (won 9–3) for a unique record.

The first pair of twins to play in an international were the Frenchmen **André and Marcel Camel** of Stade Toulouse. They played against England and Wales in 1929. Both were lock forwards, though André, who gained 15 caps from 1928–35, could also play flanker. Marcel played in three games in 1929, all defeats.

Following the Camels, twins **Stewart and James Boyce** were on the wings for Australia against New Zealand in 1964 and South Africa in 1965.

The greatest proliferation of brothers on the international pitch during the same matches are . . .

E and D James (Wales), **C E and J E Orr** and **W and G T Nielsen** (Scotland) when Scotland beat Wales at Swansea in 1892. None of the six appeared on the scoresheet.

CE and ST Meads and DB and
J Clarke (New Zealand), A and
G Boniface (France) when New
Zealand beat France 13–6 at
Auckland in 1961. Don Clarke
kicked a drop goal and two
conversions.

Gordon Brown replaced his
injured brother Peter Brown for
Scotland against Wales in 1970
at Cardiff.

Gerry, Bertie and Eddie Doran
played for Ireland between
1890–1904. Gerry and Bertie
hold an unusual statistic in that
they are the only brothers to
score international points in
different centuries!

THE McLEANS

DJ McLean won three caps for
Australia in 1904 and had four
sons, Doug, Bill, Bob and Jack.
AD 'Doug' McLean won 10
caps from 1933–6; WM 'Bill'
McLean won five caps from
1946–7; B 'Bob' McLean was an
early victim of injury; JR 'Jack'
McLean was uncapped but
toured with the 1946 Wallabies
to New Zealand.

The next generation did not let
the family down. PW McLean
was the son of Bill McLean and
won 15 caps from 1978–82;
PE McLean was the son of Bob
McLean, won 31 caps from
1974–82 and was Australia's
record holder with 261 points;
JJ McLean was another son of
Bob McLean and won 31 caps
from 1971–4.

RA McLean, who won five caps
for Australia between 1971–2,
was not related.

THE MURPHYS AND KIERNANS

Tom Kiernan won 54 caps for
Ireland from 1960–73,
captaining the 1968 British
Lions and Ireland. A points
record holder (158) and coach,
in 1988–9 he was President of
the Irish RFU.

Noel Murphy was Tom
Kiernan's cousin. He won 41
caps for Ireland between 1958
and 1969, and was also a British
Lion. He was captain of Ireland
and coach to the 1980 British
Lions. His son, Kenny Murphy,
played in all four International
Championship matches for
Ireland in 1990. Noel Murphy
senior was capped 11 times by
Ireland from 1930–3. He was
President of the Irish RFU from
1960–1.

Michael Lane was Tom Kiernan's uncle. He won 17 caps between 1947–53, and was a British Lion. **Gerald Reidy** was a cousin of Tom Kiernan. He gained five caps from 1953–4. He was also President of the Irish RFU, in 1983–4. **Michael Kiernan**, nephew of Tom Kiernan, currently has 41 caps and is the new Irish record holder with 283 points in internationals. The seven men have 172 caps between them so far, three were British Lions, and three were Presidents of the Irish RFU.

A O Morkel played against the 1903 Lions, and he, **W S Morkel** and **D T F Morkel** were all on the 1906–7 tour to Britain. WS and D T F Morkel were brothers.

W H Morkel played for South Africa in 1910. He and D T F Morkel, plus the brothers **J W H** and **P G Morkel** were all on the 1912 tour to Britain.

Five Morkels were on the tour to New Zealand in 1921. **H J Morkel**, **H W Morkel** and **J A Morkel** played in the Tests. The last to play for South Africa

was **P K Morkel** against New Zealand in 1928. The Morkels were a family of farmers from Somerset West, in South Africa Western Province.

THE BRUCE LOCKHART'S

J H Bruce Lockhart played once for Scotland in 1913 and once 1920. His brother-in-law, **H Brougham**, gained four caps for England in 1912. J H Bruce Lockhart's son, **L Bruce Lockhart**, played for Scotland on five occasions from 1948–5 and another son, **R B Bruce Lockhart**, played three times from 1937–9. The Bruce Lockharts played for London Scottish, Brougham for the Harlequins.

THE CAMBERABEROS

Guy Camberabero is the oldes – born 27 May 1936. He playe 14 times at fly-half for France from 1961–8, amassing 113 points by way of two tries, 19 conversions, 11 penalties and 1 drop goals. **Lillian Camberabero** is the brother of Guy and a year younger. He played 13 times for France between 1964–8 as scrum-half, usually partnering his brother. In his 13 matches, France lost just once.

Didier Camberabero is the eldest son of Guy – he made his debut for France in 1982, and is a current French international. In the 1987 World Cup he scored 30 points in the match against Zimbabwe, a world record. He is a fly-half but has played at full-back and on the wing. **Gilles Camberabero** is Didier's younger brother and a scrum-half. By 1990, he had yet to win a full cap but had played for France 'A' on a regular basis.

All four played for La Voulte, a small town (pop. 2500) near Valence, but Didier and Gilles moved to Beziers in 1985.

THE ELLAS

Mark Ella is the best known, twice being elected Player of the Year in Australia. He gained 25 caps between 1980–4, and retired after the Grand Slam win in Britain in 1984, having become the first to score a try in each of the four internationals. He later managed the Australian Aborigine cricket team to Britain. **Glen Ella** is Mark Ella's twin – born 5 June 1959. He played on four occasions for Australia from 1982–5 at full-

back. **Gary Ella** was born on 23 July 1960, and played four times for Australia from 1982–3 in the centre. All three brothers played for Randwick.

Steve Ella, a cousin, was a fine Australian Rugby League centre of the same era, and was in the famous 1982 Kangaroos side that created such an impression in Britain. He played in two Tests, one in 1983 and the other in 1985.

Bob Hesford (Bristol and England, 10 caps 1981–5) is part of a remarkable sporting family. Two brothers achieved excellence in other sports – **Iain Hesford** was an England Under-21 international goalkeeper and played for six league clubs including Sheffield Wednesday, Sunderland and Blackpool. **Steve Hesford** played Rugby League for Warrington and was at one stage the leading points scorer in Division One. Father **Bob Hesford** was also a First Division goalkeeper, with Huddersfield. He kept goal in the 1938 FA Cup final when Preston's Mutch scored the only goal with a penalty in the last minute of extra time.

FOR THE RECORD BOOKS

Some of the more requested but difficult to research rugby records can be found in the following lists . . .

MOST TRIES BY AN INDIVIDUAL

11 **Michel Fabre** for Beziers against Montchanin on 16 December 1979. Beziers won 100-0, and scored 21 tries (French Championship, Division 1).

Prince Obolensky was reputed to have scored **16** tries in a match on the England tour to Argentina in 1935-6.

MOST POINTS SCORED BY AN INDIVIDUAL

DUSTY HARE

Nottingham		1800
Leicester		
1976–7:	199	
1977–8:	304	
1978–9:	350	
1979–80:	319	
1980–1:	358	
1981–2:	396	
1982–3:	285	
1983–4:	239	
1984–5:	386	
1985–6:	386	
1986–7:	393	
1987–8:	374	
1988–9:	438	4427
Representative county, Barbarians, etc.		598
England internationals		240
England tours		184
British Lions		88

Total: 7337
(world record)

MOST PENALTY GOALS IN AN INTERNATIONAL

7 Hugo Porta
(Argentina) v France   1974   Buenos Aires
6 Don Clarke
(New Zealand) v British Lions   1959   Dunedin
6 Gerald Bosch
(South Africa) v France   1975   Pretoria
6 Hugo Porta
(Argentina) and
Jean Michel Aguirre
(France) in the 18–18 draw   1977   Buenos Aires
6 Gareth Evans
(Wales) v France   1982   Cardiff
6 Ollie Campbell
(Ireland) v Scotland   1982   Dublin
6 Kevin Crowley
(New Zealand) v England   1985   Christchurch
6 Gavin Hastings
(Scotland) v France   1986   Murrayfield
6 Rob Andrew
(England) v Wales   1986   Twickenham
6 Michael Lynagh
(Australia) v France   1986   Sydney
6 Grant Fox
(New Zealand) v Argentina   1987   Wellington
6 Grant Fox
(New Zealand) v Scotland   1987   Christchurch
6 Michael Lynagh
(Australia) v England   1988   Brisbane
6 Daniel Baetti
(Argentina) v France   1988   Buenos Aires

MOST CONVERSIONS IN AN INTERNATIONAL

15 Grant Fox
(New Zealand) v Japan   1987
10 Grant Fox
(New Zealand) v Fiji   1987

MOST POINTS IN AN INTERNATIONAL

30 Grant Fox
(New Zealand) v Japan   1987   15C

30 Didier Camberabero (France) v Zimbabwe	1987	3T	9C	
27 Gavin Hastings (Scotland) v Romania	1987	2T	8C	1PG
26 Alan Hewson (New Zealand) v Australia	1982	1T	2C	5PG	1DG
26 Grant Fox (New Zealand) v Fiji	1987		10C	2PG
25 Philippe Berot (France) v Romania	1987	1T	6C	3PG
24 Fergie McCormick (New Zealand) v Wales	1969		3C	5PG	1DG

MOST CONSECUTIVE TRIES IN INTERNATIONALS

8 Philippe Sella (France) in eight consecutive internationals in 1986.

6 Ian Smith (Scotland) with three tries in the second half v France in 1925, followed by three in the next game, v Wales. No other Scot scored a try to interrupt this run.

6 Ray Mordt (South Africa) three tries v New Zealand 1981, followed by three further tries against the USA in the next international.

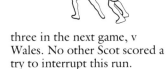

MOST DROP GOALS IN AN INTERNATIONAL

Three drop goals have been scored on a number of occasions:

Pierre Albaladejo (France) v Ireland	1960	Paris
Phil Hawthorne (Australia) v England	1967	Twickenham
Hugo Porta (Argentina) v Australia	1979	Buenos Aires
Naas Botha (South Africa) v Argentina	1980	Durban
Naas Botha (South Africa) v Ireland	1981	Durban
Jean Paul Lescarboura (France) v England	1985	Twickenham
Hugo Porta (Argentina) v New Zealand	1985	Buenos Aires
Jean Paul Lescarboura (France) v New Zealand	1986	Christchurch

MOST DROP GOALS
IN A CAREER

21 **Hugo Porta**
   (Argentina)
15 **Naas Botha**
   (South Africa)
15 **Jean Paul Lescarboura**
   (France)
12 **Pierre Albaladejo**
   (France)

MOST EXPERIENCED
INTERNATIONAL CAPTAINS

34 **Jean Pierre Rives**
   (France)
30 **Wilson Whineray**
   (New Zealand)
28 **Tom Kiernan**
   (Ireland and British Isles)

LONGEST INTERNATIONAL
CAREERS
(by season)

17	**G M Cooke** (Australia)	1932–48
16	**A J F O'Reilly** (Ireland)	1955–70
	C M H Gibson (Ireland and British Isles)	1964–79
15	**H Tanner** (Wales)	1935–49
	E E Hughes (New Zealand)	1907–21
	C E Meads (New Zealand)	1957–71
	A R Miller (Australia)	1952–67
	H Porta (Argentina)	1973–87

MOST CONSECUTIVE TESTS

53 **Willie John McBride**
   (Ireland)
53 **Gareth Edwards**
   (Wales)

THE 'CLUBS'

THE 'OVER 60' CLUB

The following have played on more than 60 occasions for their country:

81 **Mike Gibson**
   (Ireland and British Isles)
80 **Willie John McBride**
   (Ireland and British Isles)
75 **Serge Blanco**
   (France)
69 **Roland Bertranne**
   (France)
67 **Philippe Sella**
   (France)
65 **Fergus Slattery**
   (Ireland and British Isles)
63 **Gareth Edwards**
   (Wales and British Isles)
63 **J P R Williams**
   (Wales and British Isles)
63 **Benoit Dauga**
   (France)
63 **Michael Crauste**
   (France)

THE '21' CLUB

The following have scored 21 or more tries for their country:

34 **David Campese**
   (Australia)

30 **Serge Blanco**
   (France)
25 **John Kirwan**
   (New Zealand)
24 **Ian Smith**
   (Scotland and British Isles)
23 **Gerald Davies**
   (Wales and British Isles)
23 **Christian Darrouy**
   (France)
22 **Rory Underwood**
   (England)
21 **Philippe Sella**
   (France)

THE '200' CLUB

The following have scored 200 or more points for their country:

441 **Michael Lynagh**
    (Australia)
397 **Hugo Porta**
    (Argentina)
331 **Grant Fox**
    (New Zealand)
301 **Andy Irvine**
    (Scotland)
283 **Michael Kiernan**
    (Ireland)
270 **Naas Botha**
    (South Africa)
265 **Jean-Pierre Romeu**
    (France)
246 **Olly Campbell**
    (Ireland and British Isles)
240 **Dusty Hare**
    (England)
227 **Paul Thorburn**
    (Wales)
207 **Don Clarke**
    (New Zealand)
201 **Alan Hewson**
    (New Zealand)

The following have scored four or more tries in an international:

ENGLAND

5	**D Lambert** v France	1907
4	**G W Burton** v Wales	1881
4	**R W Poulton** v France	1914
4	**D M Wyatt** v USA	1977
4	**C Oti** v Romania	1989

SCOTLAND

5	**G C Lindsay** v Wales	1887
4	**W A Stewart** v Ireland	1913
4	**I S Smith** v France	1925
4	**I S Smith** v Wales	1925
4	**W B Gammell** v Japan	1977
4	**W C C Steele** v Tonga	1974
4	**I Tukalo** v Japan	1986

WALES

4	**W M Llewellyn** v England	1899
4	**R A Gibbs** v France	1908
4	**M C R Richards** v England	1969
4	**I Evans** v Canada	1987

FRANCE

4	**A Jaureguy** v Romania	1924
4	**M Celhay** v Italy	1937
4	**J B Lafond** v Japan	1985

AUSTRALIA

4 G Cornelsen v New
   Zealand   1978
4 DICampese v USA 1983

NEW ZEALAND

4 DMcGregor v England 1905
4 JJKirwan v Wales   1988
4 CIGreen v Fiji   1987
4 JAGallagher v Fiji   1987

REST OF THE WORLD
(three tries)

SMatsuo Japan v England 1979
SWalisoliso Fiji v Wales 1964

ONLY A CHILD

The following were capped at
full international level whilst still
attending school:

ENGLAND
R Richardson
Manchester Grammar   1881

FT Wright
Edinburgh Academy 1881
JG Milton
Bedford School 1904

SCOTLAND

WC Grant
Craigmount 1873
NJ Finlay
Edinburgh Academy 1875
JA Campbell
Merchiston 1878
C Reid
Edinburgh Academy 1881
M Reid
Loretto 1883
G Neilson
Merchiston 1891
W Neilson
Merchiston 1891
T Anderson
Mershiston 1882
DM Grant
Elstow, Bedford 1911

IRELAND

G McAllan
Dungannon High School 1896
JB Allison
Campbell College, Belfast 1899
EMW Harvey
Poetora 1907
FS Hewitt
Royal Institution, Belfast 1924
A Bailey
Presentation College, Bray 1934

WALES

WH Thomas
Llandovery 1885
NH Biggs
Cardiff College 1889
W Wooller
Rydal School 1933
H Tanner
Gowerton County 1935

Haydn Tanner's debut was on 21 December 1935. He was also a member of the Swansea club though still at school. On his debut he helped Wales to defeat New Zealand 13–12.

The youngest to appear for the International Rugby Board countries in full internationals are:

England **FT Wright**
18 years 8 months
Ireland **FS Hewitt**
17 years 5 months
Wales **N Biggs**
17 years 4 months
South Africa **JA Loubser**
19 years 1 month
New Zealand **E Wrigley**
19 years 3 months

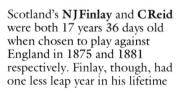

Scotland's **NJ Finlay** and **C Reid** were both 17 years 36 days old when chosen to play against England in 1875 and 1881 respectively. Finlay, though, had one less leap year in his lifetime until then and is considered the youngest.

However, the claims of **Daniel Carroll** (Australia) may need to be investigated more closely. He was 16 years 149 days old at the time of the 1908 Olympic final which was deemed an unofficial international, yet played against Wales on 12 December 1908. According to the *Guinness Book of Records*, Carroll was born on 17 February 1892, so would still have been under 17 years of age. However, the *Australian Rugby Encyclopedia* by Jack Pollard states his birthdate as 17 November 1889.

The oldest player to play international rugby was **Ned Hughes** of New Zealand, who was in the team against South Africa on 27 August 1921. He had played for New Zealand between 1907 and 1908 and had been reinstated from Rugby League in 1920. He was 40 years and 123 days old. **G E Saxby** of England was listed as 40 when he played his only game against South Africa in 1932, but it is believed that he was a year younger.

A rugby player's 'Vital Statistics' are in many ways at the discretion of the player himself. Early players were much smaller than their modern counterparts, but many of today's players prefer not to reveal details that could bring about omission from various teams, perhaps on grounds of lack of fitness. Assuming the integrity of the players, the following appear to have set records of a physical nature . . .

The first truly large rugby player, and record holder for height and weight, was **P F 'Baby' Hancock** of Blackheath and Somerset. He gained three caps for England, and went on two British Isles tours to South Africa. He was 6 ft 5 in (1.95 m) tall, and weighed 240 lb (108 kg) in 1891. By 1896 he had put on another 20 lb (9 kg). He was described as 'the king of the line out, but a real problem to fit into a scrum'.

The tallest international player is **P K Stagg** of Sale and Scotland, who gained 28 caps between 1965–70. He was 6 ft 10 in (2.05 m) and shaded **Alain Esteve** of France by an inch. **Steve Cutler** (Australia) measures 6 ft 8 in (2 m), an inch taller than **Hennie Bekker**

(South Africa), **Alejandro Iachetti** (Argentina) and **Andy Haden** (New Zealand). In some publications the New Zealander **Jock Ross** is listed at 6 ft 8 in (2 m).

The heaviest player to play international rugby is the South African prop forward **P R 'Flippie' Van der Merwe**, who gained five caps between 1981–6. He weighed in at 292 lb (132 kg) during the tour to New Zealand in 1981. Other heavyweights include **Brian Muller** (New Zealand) at 252 lb (114 kg), and Alain Esteve at 248 lb (112 kg).

The smallest player to appear in international rugby is also the lightest. The Queenslander **G H McGhie** played three times for Australia from 1928–30. He was just 5 ft 2 in (1.55 m) and weighed 128 lb (58 kg). The most resilient of the small men was **Jean Gachassin** of Lourdes and France. He gained 32 caps from 1961–9, and weighed 133 lb (60 kg). He was an inch taller than McGhie.

THREE-QUARTERS

The tallest three-quarter is believed to be **H J (Hennie) Van Zyl** of South Africa, the Transvaal wing, who played ten times for his country between 1960–1, scoring six tries. He was 6 ft 5 in (1.95 m) tall.

The heaviest three-quarter was the legendary All Black full-back **Don Clarke**, who was 245 lb (110 kg) during the later part of his international career. He was 'always fit at 17 stones' and wore size 12 boots. He played 31 Tests from 1961–4.

The largest three-quarter of the earlier era was **Pierre Faillot** of Racing Club and France who played internationally between 1911–13. Faillot was nearly 6 ft 2 in (1.85 m) and weighed 202 lb (92 kg).

FORWARDS

Forwards were smaller and lighter in the early days, when statistics were not properly kept. Two New Zealanders were particularly small – front-row forward **Bill Francis** was 5 ft 6 in (1.65 m) and flanker **Bob Wilson** weighed just under 140 lb (63.5 kg).

The French pack that played in the opening match of the 1989 International Championship would be the heaviest pack ever to take the field. Using a prop as hooker, a policy which has been in operation for several seasons, to provide an eight man shove, the tonnage of the French pack was as follows:

1 **Pascal Ondarts**
   229 lb (104 kg)
2 **Philippe Marocco**
   242 lb (110 kg)
3 **Claude Portolan**
   246 lb (112 kg)
4 **Jean Condom**
   238 lb (108 kg)
5 **Gillies Bourguignon**
   235 lb (107 kg)
6 **Alain Carminati**
   233 lb (106 kg)
7 **Marc Cecillon**
   229 lb (104 kg)
8 **Laurent Rodriquez**
   240 lb (109 kg)

Total weight
1 892 lb (860 kg)

LONGEST KICKS

PENALTIES

Until **Paul Thorburn's** monumental effort at Cardiff in 1986, little attention had been paid to measuring the distance of penalty kicks. Climatic differences can be a great aid – a gale force wind behind the kicker, or the calm, rarefied atmosphere of South Africa's High Veldt. And, unlike American Football, pitch markings are not constant, several distances having been measured by enthusiasts after the event. The following kicks are worthy of mention:

70 YARDS Paul Thorburn (Wales) v Scotland on 1 February 1986 at Cardiff. Wales won 22–15.

70 YARDS Vivian Jenkins (British Isles) v South Africa at Ellis Park, Johannesburg in 1938. South Africa won 26–12.

65 YARDS Ian McCullum (South Africa) v New Zealand at Ellis Park, Johannesburg on 12 September 1970. South Africa won 20–17.

65 YARDS Don Clarke (New Zealand) v England on 1 June 1963 at Lancaster Park, Christchurch. It was the winning kick, New Zealand triumphing 9–6.

65 YARDS Pierre Villepreux (France) v New Zealand at Athletic Park, Wellington on 27 July 1968. New Zealand won 9–3.

DROP GOALS

The 'record' for a drop goal has been estimated at 90 yards by earlier rugby books. **Gerry Brand** of South Africa was reported to have achieved the feat against England at Twickenham in 1932. Certainly it is probably the longest drop goal in history, but the distance would have to be treated with deep suspicion.

Nim Hall (England) dropped a goal from 55 yards against France on 5 April 1952, at the Stade Colombes, Paris. England won 6–3.

The greatest drop kicking exponent of the present day is **Naas Botha** of Northern Transvaal and South Africa. On his home ground at Loftus Versveld, Pretoria, and at Johannesburg, he has several times during his career dropped goals from the half-way line. It is generally agreed that Botha is the finest ever exponent of the skill.

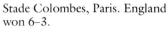

0–0 DRAWS IN INTERNATIONALS

Date		*Venue*
1885	Scotland v Wales	Hamilton Crescent, Glasgow
1886	Scotland v England	Raeburn Place, Edinburgh
1887	Wales v England	Stradey Park, Llanelli
1893	Scotland v Wales	Raeburn Place, Edinburgh
1893	Ireland v Scotland	Ballynafeigh, Belfast
1895	Ireland v Scotland	Lansdowne Road
1900	Ireland v Scotland	Lansdowne Road
1900	Scotland v England	Inverleith
1903	South Africa v British Isles	Kimberley
1910	England v Ireland	Twickenham
1921	New Zealand v South Africa	Athletic Park, Wellington
1930	England v Scotland	Twickenham
1936	Wales v England	St. Helens, Swansea
1961	France v South Africa	Stade Colombes, Paris
1962	England v Wales	Twickenham
1963	Ireland v England	Lansdowne Road
1964	Scotland v New Zealand	Murrayfield

40 POINTS OR MORE IN INTERNATIONALS

Date				*Venue*
1910	Wales	49–14	France	St. Helens, Swansea
1951	Scotland	0–44	South Africa	Murrayfield
1981	New Zealand	40–15	Scotland	Eden Park, Auckland
1985	New Zealand	42–15	England	Athletic Park, Wellington
1987	New Zealand	49–6	Wales	Brisbane
1988	New Zealand	52–3	Wales	Lancaster Park, Christchurch
1989	New Zealand	54–9	Wales	Eden Park, Auckland

MORE THAN 50 POINTS (AGGREGATE) SCORED IN ONE INTERNATIONAL

63	Wales	49–14	France	St. Helens Swansea, 1910
63	South Africa	38–25	France	Free State Stadium, Bloemfontein, 1975
63	New Zealand	54–9	Wales	Eden Park, Auckland, 1988
57	New Zealand	42–15	England	Athletic Park, Wellington, 1985
55	Wales	34–21	England	Cardiff Arms Park, 1967
55	New Zealand	40–15	Scotland	Eden Park, Auckland, 1981
55	New Zealand	49–6	Wales	Brisbane, 1987
55	New Zealand	52–3	Wales	Lancaster Park, Christchurch, 1988
55	Scotland	34–21	Ireland	Murrayfield, 1989
54	France	30–24	Australia	Concord Oval, Sydney, 1987
54	New Zealand	34–20	France	Eden Park, Auckland, 1985
52	France	13–39	England	Stade Colombes, Paris, 1914
52	South Africa	37–15	France	Loftus Versveld, Pretoria, 1980
52	Wales	18–34	Scotland	Cardiff Arms Park, 1982
51	New Zealand	38–13	Australia	Carisbrook, Dunedin, 1936
51	Australia	30–21	England	Ballymore, Brisbane, 1975
51	South Africa	33–18	France	Loftus Versveld, Pretoria, 1975
51	New Zealand	33–18	Australia	Eden Park, Auckland, 1982

BOTH TEAMS SCORING 20 POINTS OR MORE IN ONE INTERNATIONAL

Date				*Venue*
1955	South Africa	22–23	British Isles	Ellis Park, Johannesburg

Date				Venue
1967	Wales	34–21	England	Cardiff Arms Park
1968	South Africa	25–20	British Isles	Loftus Versfeld, Pretoria
1974	England	21–26	Ireland	Twickenham
1975	England	20–27	France	Twickenham
1975	Australia	30–21	England	Ballymore, Brisbane
1975	South Africa	38–25	France	Free State Stadium, Bloemfontein
1979	Wales	24–21	Ireland	Cardiff Arms Park
1980	South Africa	26–22	British Isles	Newlands, Cape Town
1981	New Zealand	25–22	South Africa	Eden Park, Auckland
1983	Scotland	25–25	New Zealand	Murrayfield
1984	Australia	24–25	New Zealand	Sydney Cricket Ground
1985	Scotland	21–25	Wales	Murrayfield
1986	England	25–20	Ireland	Twickenham
1987	France	28–22	Scotland	Parc des Princes, Paris
1987	France	20–20	Scotland	Lancaster Park, Christchurch
1987	France	30–24	Australia	Concord Oval, Sydney
1987	Wales	22–21	Australia	Rotorua International Stadium
1988	Wales	25–20	Scotland	National Stadium Cardiff
1989	Scotland	34–21	Ireland	Murrayfield
1989	New Zealand	34–20	France	Eden Park, Auckland
1989	Ireland	21–24	France	Lansdowne Road, Dublin

ENGLISH CUP

6 Bath
3 Gloucester
3 Leicester
2 Coventry
2 Gosforth
1 Bedford
1 Bristol
1 Harlequins
1 Moseley

WELSH CUP

6 Llanelli
5 Cardiff
2 Bridgend
2 Neath
1 Newport
1 Pontypool
1 Swansea
(Figures indicate number of wins)

The best international touring record is held by the 1891 British Isles tourists to South Africa. They won all 19 matches, scoring 224 points and conceding just one. A try was then worth one point. The British Isles scored 89 tries, 50 conversions, six penalty goals, four drop goals, two goals from a mark, and one penalty goal from a mark. The only point registered against the tourists was a try scored by Charles 'Hasie' Versveld in the very first match of the tour for Cape Town Clubs, who were beaten 15–1. The British Isles also won another match against Stellenbosch 2–0 but this match was regarded as unofficial.

Since then the following touring teams have remained unbeaten on a major full scale overseas tour:

British Isles
1974 to South Africa. Played 22 Won 21 Drawn 1

New Zealand
1924–5 to Britain and France. Played 30 Won 30
1967 to Britain and France. Played 15 Won 14 Drawn 1

South Africa
1971 to Australia. Played 13 Won 13

The worst major overseas full-scale touring record is held by the 1957–8 Australians to Britain and France. They played 34 matches, won 16, lost 15 and drew three. On their next visit to Britain and France the Australians won 17, lost 14 and again drew three of 34 matches.

The longest tour ever undertaken was that of the 1888–9 New Zealand team, which toured Britain and Australia. Containing Maoris and a couple of Europeans, the tourists played no fewer than 74 matches, winning 49, drawing five and losing 20. Though not described as official by the New Zealanders, the side played internationals against Ireland (won 13–4), Wales (lost 5–0) and England (lost 7–0). The full tour record of the Maoris was 107 matches played, of which they won 78, drew six and lost 23. The record includes 17 matches (all won) in New Zealand before departure, 16 matches in Australia (all won) and three others (won 1, lost 2). As the tour did not come under the NZRFU jurisdiction, no official log remains, though the tour was believed to have lasted for 21 months all told.

The most bizarre major tour would have to be that of the 1888 British tourists to Australia and New Zealand. They arrived home having lost their captain and having played two sports! The team was also sponsored by two professional cricketing greats of the time, the Englishmen Arthur Shrewsbury and Arthur Shaw. The team played nine matches in New Zealand, then went to Australia for a further 35 matches, before returning to New Zealand for the final ten matches. Unfortunately, whilst in Australia, the British team found that 19 matches were in fact

Australian Rules games! The rugby section of the tour comprised 19 games, 13 wins, four draws and two defeats. The tourists captain, R L Seddon, was drowned in a boating mishap on the Hunter River in Australia and was replaced as tour captain by A E Stoddart, another Test cricketer, who was an England international as well. Stoddart had stayed on in Australia after a cricket tour.

The best statistical record in 'junior' international rugby is that of Fiji in the 1969 South Pacific Games in Port Moresby, Papua New Guinea. In eight days, the Fijians beat Wallis and Futuna 84–8, Papua New Guinea 79–0, British Solomon Islands 113–13, New Caledonia 113–3 and in the final, Papua New Guinea 88–3. Fiji called the results 'a disaster' and offered 'sincere regret and apologies to their neighbours'.

Two major tours were called off because of the outbreak of the Second World War. The 1939 Australians reached the shores of Britain but were recalled without playing a match. In 1939, trials were held for selection for the New Zealand tour to South Africa but, again because of the outbreak of war, the tour never took place. The only international ever to take place during either World War was New Zealand's 22–7 win against Australia at the Sydney Sports Ground on 14 August 1914. Several recent tours have been cancelled because of the South African situation, whilst the South African tour to New Zealand in 1981 was severely hampered by protests. Matches in the USA on the way home were played behind closed doors.

CENTURIES

Three 'centuries' have been scored on major rugby tours – all by New Zealand:

South Australia 6 New Zealand 117
Adelaide, 11 May 1974. Tries by McLachlan (4), Batty (4), Knight (2), Karam (2), Kirkpatrick (2), D J Robertson, Callesen, Gemmell, Norton and Leslie.
Conversions by Karam (15).
Penalty Goal by Karam.
For South Australia two first-half penalty goals from Maiden.
The 78 points scored in the second half is a world record.

The next day saw the following headline on the newspaper billboards: 'New Zealand 117–6'. To which one wag had added 'South Australia to bat tomorrow'!

Japan 4 New Zealand 106
National Stadium, Tokyo,
1 November 1987.
Tries by Brooke (4), Kirwan (3),
Deans (3), Shelford (2), Brewer
(2), G Whetton, Anderson,
Fitzpatrick, Loe, McDowell.
Conversions by Fox (15).
For Japan, a try by Okidoi.
This result may, for want of a
lack of official clarification, be
the highest ever in an
international. Japan, who played
in the 1987 World Cup, fielded
a full-strength team, whilst the
entire New Zealand team were
capped internationals.

**Northern New South Wales 0
New Zealand 103**
At Quirindi on 30 May 1962.
Tries by Heeps (8), McKay (5),
Little (3), Moreton, Yates,
Graham, C E Meads, Barry and
Creighton.
Conversions by Don Clarke
(10), Briscoe (3), Yates, Barry,
Le Lievre and Ian Clarke.
Penalty goal by Don Clarke.
In modern terms the score
would have been 125–0, and the
score is still a world record for
the number of tries. Rod Heeps'
eight tries is a record for a player
on tour. Heeps and McKay's
total of 13 tries is a record for
two wings in a match.

ATTENDANCES

The world record for an
international match is 104000

for the Scotland v Wales match
in Edinburgh on 1 March 1975.

On 19 May 1957 a crowd of
95000 was reported at the
Romania v France match at
Bucharest's August 23rd
Stadium. The figure was
reported to be accurate but it
was claimed that most were
football supporters waiting to
watch a match against Poland. In
fact, the football match was a 'B'
International, so most would
have been rugby supporters.

In the famous First Test of the
1955 British Lions tour to South
Africa which the tourists won
23–22, a crowd of 95000 was
present.

With crowd safety rightly a
major issue, these figures may
not now be approached, with
the exception of the new Ellis
Park Stadium in Johannesburg.
The capacity is 104000 – all
seated.

The smallest attendance at an
international rugby match is
2000 which occurred on two
occasions: England v Wales at

Cardigan Fields, Leeds on 5 January 1884 and Scotland v Wales at Hamilton Crescent, Glasgow on 10 January 1885.

The smallest attendance at a rugby international in modern times is 4800 at Brisbane Cricket Ground to witness New Zealand beat Australia 16–6 on 21 July 1951.

Capacities of some of the major International Rugby centres in 1990 (subject to safety control)

Twickenham	69 500
National Stadium, Cardiff	64 500
Murrayfield	70 000
Lansdowne Road, Dublin	50 000
Eden Park, Auckland	49 000
Lancaster Park, Christchurch	42 500
Carisbrook, Dunedin	37 500
Athletic Ground, Wellington	42 000
Ellis Park, Johannesburg	104 000
Loftus Versveld, Pretoria	72 000
Newlands, Cape Town	58 500
Kings Park, Durban	58 000
Free State Stadium, Bloemfontein	48 000
Boet Erasmus Stadium, Port Elizabeth	46 500
Sydney Cricket Ground	49 850
Ballymore, Brisbane	25 000
Concord Oval, Sydney	22 000
Parc des Princes, Paris	49 000
Velez Sarsfield, Buenos Aires	52 000
National Stadium, Tokyo	62 500
Hilversum, Holland	23 000
Burnaby, Vancouver	22 000
23rd August, Bucharest	75 000
National Stadium, Suva	25 000

Several unofficial claims to the highest attendance at a club match have been reported. On 21 November 1953, a crowd of 56 000 saw the Cardiff v New Zealand match at Cardiff Arms Park. Cardiff beat the tourists 8–3. The Barbarians are a club in the strictest sense of the word, and their farewell matches against the departing tourists have seen several attendances of 60 000.

The first capacity Schweppes Cup final took place at the National Stadium, Cardiff between Llanelli and Neath on 7 May 1988, with Llanelli winning 28–13. The attendance was 56 500. The highest attendance for a friendly between two club sides is 48 500 between Cardiff and Newport at the Cardiff Arms Park in 1950–1.

It should be noted that on several occasions the Japanese final between the University sides of Doshiba, Keio and Washeda has been played before a capacity crowd of 62 500.

THE INTERNATIONAL GROUNDS

The following stadia have all hosted matches between International Board countries:

SCOTLAND

Raeburn Place, Edinburgh
Hamilton Crescent, Glasgow
Old Hampden Park, Glasgow
Powderhall, Edinburgh
Inverleith, Edinburgh
Hampden Park, Glasgow
Murrayfield, Edinburgh

ENGLAND

Kennington Oval, London
Whalley Range, Manchester
Rectory Field, Blackheath
Cardigan Fields, Leeds
Birkenhead Park
Crown Flatt, Dewsbury
Athletic Ground, Richmond
Headingley, Leeds
Meanwood Road, Leeds
Fallowfield, Manchester
Kingsholm, Gloucester
Welford Road, Leicester
Crystal Palace, London
Ashton Gate, Bristol
Twickenham

WALES

St Helen's, Swansea
Rodney Parade, Newport
Arms Park, Cardiff (now
    National Stadium)
Stradey Park, Llanelli

IRELAND

Ormeau, Belfast
Lansdowne Road, Dublin
Ballynafeigh, Belfast
Balmoral, Belfast
Limerick
Mardyke, Cork
Ravenhill, Belfast

AUSTRALIA

Sydney Cricket Ground
Woollongabba, Brisbane
Sydney Sports Ground
Brisbane Cricket Ground
Exhibition Ground, Brisbane
Lang Park, Brisbane
Ballymore Oval, Brisbane
Concord Oval, Sydney

SOUTH AFRICA

Crusader Ground, Port
    Elizabeth
Griqualand West Stadium,
    Kimberley
Newlands, Cape Town
Wanderers Ground,
    Johannesburg
Kingsmead, Durban
Ellis Park, Johannesburg
Boet Erasmus Stadium, Port
    Elizabeth
Free State Stadium,
    Bloemfontein
Loftus Versveld Stadium,
    Pretoria
Kings Park, Durban
Pam Brink Stadium, Springs

FRANCE

Parc des Princes, Paris
Stade Colombes, Paris

Stade Bouscat, Bordeaux
Stade Pershing, Paris
Stade des Ponts Jumeaux,
   Toulouse
Stade Yves du Manoir, Paris
Stade de Toulouse
Stade Marcel Michelen,
   Clermont Ferrand
Stade Beaujoire, Nantes
Stade de Meinau, Strasbourg
Stade Grimpooris, Lille

NEW ZEALAND

Athletic Park, Wellington
Tahuna Park, Dunedin
Carisbrook, Dunedin
Potters Park, Auckland
Lancaster Park, Christchurch
Eden Park, Auckland
Epsom Showgrounds, Auckland
International Stadium, Rotorua

The table below shows the date
of the first international played
at each stadium:

Date of
first
International   *Ground*

27	Mar	1871	Raeburn Place, Edinburgh
5	Feb	1872	Kennington Oval, London
3	Mar	1873	Hamilton Crescent, Glasgow
19	Feb	1877	Ormeau, Belfast
28	Feb	1880	Whalley Range, Manchester
19	Feb	1881	Rectory Field, Blackheath
28	Jan	1882	Lansdowne Road, Dublin
16	Dec	1882	St Helen's, Swansea
5	Jan	1884	Cardigan Fields, Leeds
12	Jan	1884	Rodney Parade, Newport
12	Apr	1884	Arms Park, Cardiff
8	Jan	1887	Stradey Park, Llanelli
12	Mar	1887	Birkenhead Park
15	Feb	1890	Crown Flatt, Dewsbury
21	Feb	1891	Ballynafeigh, Belfast
7	Mar	1891	Athletic Ground, Richmond
30	Jul	1891	Crusader Ground, Port Elizabeth
28	Aug	1891	Griqualand West Stadium, Kimberley
5	Sep	1891	Newlands, Cape Town
4	Mar	1893	Headingley, Leeds
1	Feb	1896	Meanwood Road, Leeds
14	Mar	1896	Old Hampden Park, Glasgow
22	Aug	1896	Wanderers Ground, Johannesburg
20	Feb	1897	Powderhall, Edinburgh
13	Mar	1897	Fallowfield, Manchester
19	Feb	1898	Balmoral Showgrounds, Belfast

Date of first International	Ground
18 Mar 1898	Limerick
18 Feb 1899	Inverleith, Edinburgh
6 Jan 1900	Kingsholm, Gloucester
8 Feb 1902	Welford Road, Leicester
15 Aug 1903	Sydney Cricket Ground
13 Aug 1904	Athletic Park, Wellington
11 Feb 1905	Mardyke, Cork
2 Sep 1905	Tahuna Park, Dunedin
2 Dec 1905	Crystal Palace, London
1 Jan 1906	Parc des Princes, Paris
17 Nov 1906	Hampden Park, Glasgow
3 Aug 1907	Woollongabba Ground, Brisbane
1 Jan 1908	Stade de Colombes, Paris
18 Jan 1908	Ashton Gate, Bristol
6 Jan 1908	Carisbrook, Dunedin
25 Jun 1908	Potters Park, Auckland
15 Jan 1910	Twickenham
11 Jan 1913	Stade Bouscat, Bordeaux
20 Sep 1913	Lancaster Park, Christchurch
18 Jul 1914	Sydney Sports Ground
1 Aug 1914	Brisbane Cricket Ground
27 Aug 1921	Eden Park, Auckland
1 Jan 1924	Stade Pershing, Paris
9 Feb 1924	Ravenhill, Belfast
16 Aug 1924	Kingsmead, Durban
18 Jan 1925	Stade des Ponts Jumeaux, Toulouse
21 Mar 1925	Murrayfield
21 Jul 1928	Ellis Park, Johannesburg
30 Dec 1928	Stade Yves du Manoir, Paris
20 Jul 1929	Brisbane Exhibition Ground
26 Aug 1933	Boet Erasmus Stadium, Port Elizabeth
2 Sep 1933	Free State Stadium, Bloemfontein
3 Sep 1955	Loftus Versveld, Pretoria
20 Sep 1958	Epsom Showgrounds, Auckland
23 May 1964	Kings Park, Durban
25 Jul 1964	Pam Brink Stadium, Springs, South Africa
26 Jun 1965	Lang Park, Brisbane
22 Jun 1968	Ballymore Oval, Brisbane
20 Nov 1971	Stade de Toulouse
13 Nov 1983	Stade Marcel Michelen, Clermont-Ferrand
15 Nov 1986	Stade de Beaujoire, Nantes
21 Jun 1986	Concord Oval, Sydney
18 Jun 1987	International Stadium, Rotorua
4 Nov 1989	Stade de Meinau, Strasbourg
11 Nov 1989	Stade Grimpooris, Lille

REFEREES

The first major refereeing incident was so controversial that it led to the formation of the International Board. Referee George Scriven of Ireland, who had played international rugby the previous season as captain of Ireland, allowed an England score, which came from a 'knock back' by a Scot, during the international between the two countries at the Rectory Field, Blackheath, on 1 March 1884. Dr Scriven's decision to award the try (after 10 minutes of on-the-field discussion) and the fact that it was converted for an England win so incensed the Scots that they cancelled fixtures with England. The case went to the highest justice in the land.

The 'Deans incident' which has sent New Zealanders and Welshmen into conflict every time the episode is mentioned occurred at Cardiff Arms Park on 16 December 1905. The crux of the story concerned whether R G Deans, the Canterbury centre, reached the line before being tugged back. The score was disallowed and New Zealand, a try behind at that stage, eventually lost their only match of the tour by that score. Deans claimed on his deathbed that he scored; most of Wales thought he didn't but folklore has built up around the incident, so much so that New Zealand tours always visit the spot! The referee, John Dewar Dallas, had played international rugby for Scotland against England in 1903. At 27 years of age he was younger than eight of the players on the field!

R W Jeffares, the son of the Secretary of the Irish Rugby Football Union, refereed Ireland's international with New Zealand in 1935. The original choice, W A Allan of Scotland, was still at sea, sheltering from a storm, when the game kicked off in Dublin. New Zealand won 17–9.

Colonel John Brunton delayed the kick-off of the Wales v New Zealand game at Swansea on 29 November 1924, because he was unhappy with the state of the match ball. He similarly rejected two more given to him, and the match commenced with the fourth new ball.

Robert Calmet, the French referee, was caught in a ruck just before half time in the England v Wales match at Twickenham on 28 February 1970. He was replaced by the English international touch judge RF'Johnny' Johnson. Calmet was found to have broken his leg. In the meantime Mr Johnson officiated through a 13–3 English lead to a 17–13 Welsh victory!

Another Frenchman, Dr Cuny, aged 48, badly injured a leg muscle half an hour from the end of the Wales v Scotland match on 7 February 1975. Despite pleas for him to leave the field, he hobbled around at least 40 yards behind the play, which degenerated into chaos. Wales won 28–6, but the unfortunate Dr Alain Cuny found that his first international was also his last.

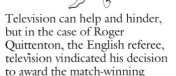

Television can help and hinder, but in the case of Roger Quittenton, the English referee, television vindicated his decision to award the match-winning

penalty to New Zealand against Wales on 11 November 1978 at Cardiff. Wales, who had not beaten New Zealand since 1953 – the series continued – claimed that the referee had fallen for a blatant dive by Andy Haden from a line-out in the last few seconds. However, evidence showed that just prior to the Haden incident, Mr Quittenton had already blown for barging by Geoff Wheel on the tourists' lock Frank Oliver.

On the 1888–9 tour to Britain, the New Zealand Maoris were brought to a halt during the match against Yorkshire (which they won 10–6) by the sight of John Cail, the referee, disappearing into the crowd to find a watch after his had failed.

The tallest referee may well have been Montagu Arnold of Australia. He refereed the New South Wales v Queensland match in 1882. Mr Arnold was 6 ft 6 in (1.98 m) tall, the tallest on the field, and was selected to 'knock some discipline into the players'.

Dr Wheeler, the Irish referee, overruled his touch judges during the England v Wales game on 17 February 1931. Both touch judges deemed the kick had failed, but the start of the second half was delayed whilst Dr Wheeler ordered the scoreboard to be altered. England led 8–6 with the incident but Wales, who had never won at Twickenham at that stage, drew 11–11.

Referee John Reardon had to stop the England v Mid-West encounter at Cleveland, Ohio, on 13 June 1982, early in the second half with England fluently involved in what would have been a further try (England won 53–7). Reardon explained that he was under orders to stop because the local television station was screening adverts!

Adrian Stoop, the former Harlequins and England half-back, took up refereeing after being wounded in the First World War. During the 1921 East Midlands v Barbarians game at Northampton, Stoop blew for full time 14 minutes early. The players and referee were brought back from the bath to complete the match.

John Coffey gained the last of his 19 caps for Ireland against France in Paris in 1910. Less then two years later he was refereeing France's international with Scotland. Before the rules of rugby were properly drawn up, current internationals used to referee other internationals, but Coffey's change from jersey to whistle at international level represents a modern record.

Maritz Nel, younger brother of Philip Nel, the South African captain on the 1937 tour to New Zealand, collided with referee Theo Pienaar in the 1928 South African trials, and was admitted to hospital for five days.

In the France v Wales match on 27 March 1965, the referee R W Gilliland of Ireland burst a blood vessel in his calf after 32 minutes and was assisted from the field. His replacement was the Frenchman Bernard Marie, acting touch judge, who had refereed the Wales v Fiji match a year earlier.

Two drop goals that were given in the same match evened up controversies. Referee Mike Titcomb of Bristol gave a Mike Gibson drop goal to Ireland which was clearly touched in flight by a Welsh hand, while Ireland lined up for a drop-out when Gareth Edwards' effort seemed to have passed by a post. The match in Dublin on 9 March 1968 finished Ireland 9 Wales 6.

On 14 March 1936 the English referee Cyril Gadney turned up to referee the Wales v Ireland match. Wales were in line for the championship and Ireland could have won the Triple Crown, so there was a huge crowd. When Mr Gadney presented himself at

the entrance he was told in no uncertain terms that he was at least the 100th person to have attempted to enter the ground by pretending to be the referee. With the clock moving towards kick-off time, the referee was eventually found by embarrassed members of the Welsh RU in a queue in Westgate Street, paying to get in. Wales won 3–0.

In the first Test between New Zealand and South Africa at Wellington in 1937, photos clearly depict L E Macassey, the referee, jumping into the air in celebration after a fine drop goal by Trevathan had sewn up a New Zealand win by 13–7. It should be recorded that Trevathan and Macassey were neighbours in Otago.

In 1973 English referee Ken Pattinson had to retire after 13 minutes of the France v Scotland international on 13 January at the Parc des Princes. Luckily the reserve, and touch judge for the match, was a referee destined to become one of the most respected in world rugby – François Palmade, who, according to the Scots, was 'a most impartial and strict referee'. France won 16–13 in the first match at the Parc des Princes.

Below is an ever-growing list of all those who have been sent off in international matches . . .

Cyril Brownlie (New Zealand) by referee Albert Freethy (Wales) in tenth minute of the match against England at Twickenham on 18 January 1925. Brownlie was not suspended as it was the last match of the tour.

Colin Meads (New Zealand) by referee Kevin Kelleher (Ireland) four minutes from the end of the match against Scotland at Murrayfield on 2 December 1967. Meads was suspended for two matches.

Mike Burton (England) by referee R T Burnett (Australia) after two minutes of the match against Australia in Brisbane on 31 May 1975. Burton was cautioned; it was the last match of the tour.

Geoff Wheel (Wales) and **Willie Duggan** (Ireland) after 38

minutes on 15 January 1977 by referee Norman Sanson (Scotland). Both players were suspended.

Paul Ringer (Wales) by referee David Burnett (Ireland) after 13 minutes of the match against England at Twickenham on 16 February 1980. Ringer was suspended for six weeks.

Jean-Pierre Garuet (France) by referee Clive Norling (Wales) after 62 minutes of the match against Ireland on 21 January 1984. Garuet was suspended for the rest of the season.

Huw Richards (Wales) by referee Kerry Fitzgerald (Australia) after 77 minutes of the World Cup semi-final against New Zealand in Brisbane on 14 June 1987.

David Codey (Australia) by referee Fred Howard (England) after four minutes of the World Cup third place play-off match against Australia at Rotorua (NZ) on 18 June 1987.

Mosose Taga (Fiji) by referee Kerry Fitzgerald (Australia) in the 67th minute of the game against England on 17 June 1988.

Alain Lorieux (France) by referee Owen Doyle (Ireland) in the 78th minute against Argentina in Buenos Aires on 26 June 1988.

Tevita Vonulagi and **Noa Nadruku** (Fiji) by referee Brian Stirling (Ireland) in separate incidents during the second half of the match against England at Twickenham on 4 November 1989. Both were banned for a month.

Kevin Moseley (Wales) by referee Fred Howard (England) after 32 minutes of the Wales v France game at Cardiff on 17 January 1990. He was suspended for seven months.

Alain Carminati (France), also by referee Fred Howard after 49 minutes of the Scotland v France match at Murrayfield on 20 February 1990. He too was suspended for seven months.

ALL-ROUNDERS: RUGBY PLAYERS' OTHER SPORTS

Eric Liddell, of *Chariots of Fire* fame, was a double international. His career has been chronicled in the Oscar-winning film, together with Harold Abrahams'. Liddell's first passion was rugby; he gained seven caps for Scotland between 1922–4, his speed enabling him to score four tries for his country.He then gave up rugby to concentrate on athletics. He won a gold medal in the 400 metres and a bronze in the 200 metres at the Paris Olympics of 1924. Because of his beliefs he

id not run in a potential gold
medal-winning sprint relay team,
or the 100 metres. He was the
British record holder for 100
yards at 9.7 seconds. Born in
China in 1902, he came to
Scotland at the age of five. He
died in a Japanese internment
camp on 21 February 1945.

Morris Kirksey won a gold
medal in the sprint relay at the
1920 Olympics and a silver in
the 100 metres after winning
gold in the Olympic rugby final.
(*See Olympic Rugby, page 27*)

Two other rugby internationals
won Olympic silver medals. **Ken
Jones**, the 44-times capped
Welsh wing and 1950 British
Lion, ran the anchor leg in
Britain's sprint relay team which
took the silver medals at the
1948 Olympics. The second leg
was run by **Jack Gregory** of
England who gained his only
cap for England against Wales
(and Ken Jones) in 1949. For an
hour both Jones and Gregory
had gold medals – the winning
USA team were disqualified,
then eventually reinstated to the
gold medal position.

There have been several national
sprint champions who have been
rugby internationals over the
years, but the only rugby player
to have won international caps
and Commonwealth Games
sprint titles was **C B Holmes**.
The Manchester University
student won the 100 and 220
yards at the 1938
Commonwealth Games, then at
the age of 31 played for England
against Scotland in 1947, scoring
a try, and against Ireland and
France in 1948.

George Smith of Auckland was a
rugby international and world
athletics record holder. He
gained two caps for New Zealand
on the memorable 1905 tour to
Britain, against Scotland (two
tries) and Ireland. He scored 34
tries in just 39 games for the All
Blacks on tour. He won 15 New
Zealand athletics titles, and in
1904 set a world record time of
58.5 seconds for the 440 yards
hurdles.

BOXERS

**Few boxers of repute have
played rugby at top level,
though several notable
hardmen in the forwards have
shown considerable ring skills
. . .**

Snowy Baker won the silver
medal in the middleweight

division of the 1908 Olympics, being narrowly outpointed by the future England cricket captain J W H T Douglas. Baker won two Rugby Union caps for Australia in 1904.

Arturo Rodriquez Jurado won the 1928 Olympic heavyweight title, and played rugby for the Argentine club champions CA San Isidro. He also played for the national side, though the Pumas were not then the world force they are now.

Tom Heeney, lock forward against South Africa in 1921 for Hawkes Bay/Poverty Bay, later went on to lose to Gene Tunney in the 11th round of a world heavyweight title fight in 1928.

Joe Erskine, the British heavyweight champion involved in epic fights with Henry Cooper, Brian London and Dick Richardson, was the Welsh Schools' fly-half in his younger days.

Kallie Knoetze, the South African heavyweight who fought John Tate in a 1979 world heavyweight title fight eliminator and was ranked number two in the world at one time, played in the back row for the powerful and successful Northern Transvaal XV in many Currie Cup successes.

Jerry Shea (Newport and Wales, four caps 1919–21) was a professional boxer. Though never a champion, he fought several world-ranked opponents. On 20 February 1920, whilst a current rugby international, he fought Ted Kid Lewis at Mountain Ash and was stopped in the first round. Lewis had lost his world welterweight title the previous year.

CRICKETERS

Eric William Thomas Tindall is unique. He is the only person to play international rugby and Test cricket, then become both an international rugby referee and a Test match umpire. Tindall was born on 18 December 1910, and was educated at Wellington College. He played provincial rugby for Wellington as first five-eighth, and was chosen to tour Britain with the 1935–6 All Blacks. He was capped against England in what became known as Obolensky's match. Altogether he played in 17 tour matches in

Britain and Australia for the All Blacks. In summer, Tindall was a wicketkeeper for Wellington from 1933–50, playing in five Test matches for New Zealand from 1937–47. As with his rugby career he toured both England and Australia.

After retiring from the playing side, Tindall took up refereeing and umpiring. He refereed both the first and second Tests against the 1950 British Lions tourists, and the second Test against Australia in 1955. As an umpire he stood in the 1959 Test between New Zealand and England. His international career began with being on the receiving end of Obolensky's two famous tries, and ended with Ted Dexter's 141 and Tony Lock's match figures of 11 for 84, in an England team which also contained Graveney, Cowdrey, May, Tyson and Trueman. Not surprisingly, his two sons were both good enough to play rugby for Wellington.

CAPTAIN OF COUNTRY AT BOTH RUGBY AND CRICKET

Two Englishmen and a South African have captained their countries at both Rugby Union and cricket:

A N Hornby was the first to captain his country at both

sports. He was England's cricket captain in the Test match which is now world famous as the Ashes Test, the Australian press having pronounced English cricket 'dead' after the match! Hornby batted number 10 in the first innings and opened in the second! Australia won the match by seven runs in 1882 at the Oval. In all he played three Tests for England, two as captain, and failed to reach double figures with the bat! His bowling was better, though. He bowled for one spell only and achieved seven overs, seven maidens and a wicket. He scored 15 centuries in his Lancashire career. He played Rugby Union for Manchester and England, being capped by England on seven occasions between 1877–82. He was captain for his last international v Scotland.

A E Stoddart also captained England at both Rugby Union and cricket. As a cricketer he was one of the finest, opening the batting for England with W G Grace. He played in 16 Tests, eight as captain, and scored 996 Test runs at 35.56, with two centuries. His 173 v Australia was an English record at the time. He made 26 centuries in his career for Middlesex and England, and also held the world club record of 485 runs for Hampstead v Stoics.

As a rugby player, he gained 11 caps for England from 1885–93 with the Blackheath club, being captain on several occasions. But his rugby captaincies may be better known for the wrong reasons; it was he who assumed the captaincy of the 1888 British Isles team when WL Seddon was drowned in a boating accident on the Hunter River in Australia (*see page 55*).

ARRichards captained South Africa in his only cricket Test v England in 1896, twice being dismissed by another dual international, SMJWoods. Prior to that he had played in all three rugby Tests against the 1891 British Isles tourists, being captain for the last match. When the British Isles returned in 1896, he refereed the first Test.

DUAL INTERNATIONALS WHO WERE WERE CAPTAINS IN ONE SPORT

JHAnderson captained South Africa in his only cricket Test match in 1902 against Australia, who won by 159 runs. Anderson made 32 and 11. He had earlier played all three Tests against the 1896 British Isles rugby team. Anderson was a Western Province centre.

HOOwen Smith played in all five cricket Tests against England for South Africa in 1929, scoring a superb 129 in the second Test. Staying in England to study, he played rugby for Oxford University and St Mary's Hospital, gaining 10 caps and captaining England from full-back.

MJKSmith played 50 Tests for England and was captain in 25 of them. He scored 2278 Test runs at 31.63 with three centuries and over 30 000 runs in first class cricket. His Test cricket career spanned the years 1958–72, considerably longer than his only rugby cap for England v Wales in 1956 at Twickenham. Smith was England's fly-half; Wales won 8–3.

DUAL RUGBY AND CRICKET INTERNATIONALS

AWPowell was a one-cap wonder for South Africa in cricket and rugby – in 1898–9 he was top scorer with 11 in South Africa's paltry 35 all out in his only cricket Test, having previously played against the British Isles rugby team in the third Test which the tourists won 9–3. He played for Griqualand West.

PSTJones fared better at rugby than cricket. The Western

Province player played three times against the 1896 British Isles rugby team for South Africa. His only Test cricket appearance was a disaster – against Australia in 1902–3 he was out without scoring in both innings.

J H Sinclair hit South Africa's first three Test centuries including a Botham-style six sixes in his 104 against England in 1902–3. He played 25 times for South Africa, scoring 1 069 rapid runs and taking 63 wickets from 1896–1911. As a forward for Transvaal he gained one cap in the 10–10 draw for South Africa against the 1903 British Isles team.

R H Spooner played 10 times for England at cricket between 1905–12, making 112 v South Africa in 1912. He also played on the wing for his only cap for England in the 21–5 defeat by Wales in 1903.

T A Harris was one of South Africa's finest rugby players of his time. He was a star in the famous 1937 series win in New Zealand and also played fly-half against the 1938 British Lions. He gained five caps. After the war, he played three cricket Tests with a highest score of 60 at Trent Bridge on his Test debut.

G F Vernon was another one-cap wonder in two sports. He played in the nine-wicket loss to Australia in 1882–3 and was in England's rugby team for the first Calcutta Cup match at Blackheath against Scotland in 1878.

DUAL INTERNATIONALS BUT FOR DIFFERENT COUNTRIES

W H Milton played rugby for England against Scotland in 1874. He then moved to South Africa and played three cricket Tests, two as captain, and all against England. In his first match as captain South Africa were bowled out for 47 and 43 in 1888–9, and in his final match as captain England again won, by an innings and 202 runs! He played rugby for Marlborough Nomads.

F Mitchell played cricket for England on two occasions in 1898–9, opening the batting with P F Warner. Earlier, in 1895–6, he had gained six caps as a member of the England pack. Mitchell, of Cambridge

University, Blackheath, and Yorkshire CCC, then captained South Africa in three 1912 cricket Tests.

CB Van Reyneveld played cricket for South Africa on 19 occasions from 1951–8, eight times as captain. In 1948–9 he played all four Five Nations championship matches in the centre for England.

S M J Woods played three times for Australia (1888) and three times for England (1895–6) at cricket. He was a fine forward for England, playing 13 times between 1890–5.

RO Schwarz played three times for England from 1899–1901 while a Richmond RFC member. He then went on to play 20 cricket Tests for South Africa, with best figures of 6 for 47 amongst 55 Test wickets at 25.76. He took South Africa's first Test wicket.

R H M Hands, the Oxford University and Blackheath forward, gained two caps for

England from 1910–13. He then played for South Africa in his only cricket Test against England and was out stumped in both innings. Such irresponsibility cost him any more caps!

M P Donnelly was one of the world's finest left-handed batsmen, as befits a Test batting average for New Zealand of 52.90 which included a superb 206 v England at Lord's in 1949. It may have come as revenge for England dropping the Oxford and Canterbury utility back after his only England rugby cap in the 22–0 débâcle v Ireland in 1947.

M K Elgie of London Scottish played eight times for Scotland in 1954–5. Emigrating to South Africa, he made his Test cricket debut at the same time as Colin Bland, Eddie Barlow and Peter Pollock. He played three cricket Tests.

C MacGregor was England's wicketkeeper in eight Tests from 1890–3, and was an outstanding full-back and centre of his day, playing 13 times for Scotland from 1890–5.

M J L Turnbull played nine times for England's cricket team whilst with Glamorgan CCC from 1930–6. He was a fine scrum-half for Cardiff in the winter months, and gained two caps for Wales in 1933 – against Ireland, and in Wales's historic first-ever win at Twickenham, 9–3 against England.

Born 6 November 1953, **Brian John McKechnie** is a quiz questioner's delight. He is the nearest in recent years to a dual international, having played both cricket and rugby for New Zealand. However, he has only played in one-day internationals for the cricket side. The other intriguing aspect of McKechnie is that he was involved in two controversial issues of the day. In 1978 he kicked the match-winning penalty against Wales after Andy Haden had clearly 'dived' to secure it (referee Quittenton had correctly blown for another infringement, but you tell that to the Welsh!) and in his one-day international cricket career he was the recipient of the underarm ball bowled by Australia's Trevor Chappell under orders from his brother Greg, the captain.

Alan Walker the New South Wales centre played in the 1947–8 Wallabies tour to Britain, but did not make the Test team. As a cricketer Walker went on the 1949–50 tour to South Africa but did not make that Test team either! As a fast bowler for Nottinghamshire against Leicestershire in 1956, he took four wickets in four balls – the last in the Leicestershire first innings, and a hat-trick with the first three balls of their second innings.

Wilfred Wooller (Cardiff and Wales, 18 caps 1933–9) was captain of Glamorgan County Cricket Club from 1947–60. He played for the county from 1938–62, scoring 12 078 runs and taking 892 wickets in a career that brought him close to Test selection.

Alan Rees (Maesteg and Wales, three caps 1962) was a regular member of the Glamorgan CCC middle order batting from 1955–68, scoring 7 681 runs at 24.07 with two centuries and 36 fifties.

Rob Andrew (Wasps and England's most capped fly-half with 25 caps up to 1990) played first class cricket for Cambridge University – and was captain of both rugby and cricket in 1985. He scored an unbeaten 101 v

Nottinghamshire in 1984.

Another player close to dual international recognition in recent years was **Alistair Hignell** (Bristol and England, 15 caps 1975–9) who played cricket for Gloucestershire from 1974–83. He scored 7459 runs at an average of 30 with 11 first class centuries. He was often mentioned in the media as a potential England cricketer, but retired at the age of 28.

Gerbrand Grobler (Northern Transvaal, born 10 August 1962) has played in both the Currie Cup cricket final as an all-rounder, and the Currie Cup rugby final as a full back for Northern Transvaal (1987–9).

Dusty Hare – the world points record holder – was also an accomplished cricketer. He played for Nottinghamshire from 1971–7, and once shared a century stand with Garfield Sobers against Warwickshire at Coventry in 1974 when he made his top score of 36.

FOOTBALL

It is obviously more difficult to play two winter sports at full

international level, but there are some who have managed to play both rugby and soccer at top level:

Kevin O'Flanagan gained seven football caps for the Republic of Ireland while with Bohemians up to 1938. After the Second World War he added another three caps whilst with Arsenal (14 league games) and Brentford (six league games). As a member of London Irish he played Rugby Union for Ireland against Australia in 1947.

Michael O'Flanagan, Kevin's brother, was a 'one-cap wonder' in rugby and soccer. A member of the Lansdowne club, he played football against England in 1946 alongside Kevin (against a team that included Swift, Wright, Finney, Carter, Lawton and Mannion, and lost only 1–0), and then played against Scotland in the 1948 British International championship.

Three other dual rugby and soccer internationals played in the last century. **R H Birkett** (Clapham Rovers) played in the first ever rugby international between England and Scotland in 1871, and gained four caps in all. He also played football for England v Scotland in 1879.

CP Wilson (Marlborough Nomads and England) played rugby against Wales in 1881, and when with Hendon played twice for the England football team in 1884, against Scotland and Wales.

J W Sutcliffe (Bolton and Millwall) played five times for the England football team from 1893–1903, and in 1889 played for the England rugby team against New Zealand.

David Johnston (Watsonians and Scotland, 27 caps 1979–86)

was a professional with Hearts before turning to rugby. He played 11 games in the Scottish First Division. As a junior he was on the books of Meadowbank Thistle and Glasgow Rangers.

MISCELLANEOUS

Stanley Harris of Blackheath played twice for England in 1920. He then moved to Johannesburg and was recalled to national colours when the British Isles toured South Africa in 1924, playing in the third and fourth Tests of the series.

Harris also played lawn tennis. He was in South Africa's Davis Cup team, and also won the All

England mixed doubles title. He played polo for England. He was also selected for two sports for South Africa in the 1924 Olympics – boxing and the modern pentathlon. Almost as an afterthought, he also reached the final of the World Ballroom Dancing Championships.

Noel Purcell of Ireland won a gold medal as part of the Great Britain water polo team at the 1920 Antwerp Olympics. On 12 February 1921 he gained the first of four caps for Ireland in the back row. Purcell played for Lansdowne.

CB Fry pulled a hamstring just before the start of the 1895 Varsity match, an injury which probably cost him an England rugby cap. Oxford won the university match, with half the side being picked to play for England in the next international. Fry held the world long jump record for 25 years with a leap of 23 ft 6 in (7.15 m), and scored only 114 runs short of 40 000 in first class cricket for an average of 50.22. He captained England at cricket on several occasions and played football for Southampton as far back as the 1901 FA Cup final, also gaining two caps for England. At rugby, though, he played for the best team in the land, Blackheath, and the Barbarians, but still missed out on that elusive cap.

In 1890 and 1893 **FO Stoker** and **J Pim** won the men's doubles in the All England Championships at Wimbledon. In 1891 the pair were runners-up. In 1886 FO Stoker of Wanderers gained the first of five caps that he won in the back row and front row for Ireland.

JP 'Pringle' Fisher, who gained a place in the Great Britain basketball team at the 1960 Olympic Games in Rome, was one of Scotland's finest back row forwards with 25 caps.

Roger Cornforth of Australia, who gained two caps, one in 1947 and the other against the 1950 British Isles, also represented his country at water polo at the 1956 Olympics in Melbourne.

David Marques (Harlequins and England, 23 caps 1956–61) was a crewman on the yacht *Sovereign* which lost to *Constellation* 4–0 in the 1964 America's Cup challenge.

Frank Luscombe (Gipsies and England, six caps 1872–6)

owned several famous racehorses, even in his playing days. He later owned two Cambridgeshire winners, Marco (1895) and Marcovil (1905).

Henry Kayll (Sunderland and England, one cap 1878) was the then English pole vault champion, and set a possible world's best vault of 11 ft 1 in (3.35m) in 1877.

Peter Howard (Old Milhillians, Oxford University and England, eight caps 1930–1) was a member of the 1938 British four-man bobsleigh world championship team. His wife Doris was 1932 Wimbledon ladies' doubles champion with Josane Sigart of Belgium.

Aubrey Dowson (Moseley and England, one cap 1899) was a member of the New College Oxford rowing eight which won the blue riband event at Henley in 1897 – the Grand Challenge Cup.

Marshall Brooks (Oxford University and England, one cap 1874) set a world's best high jump of 6 ft 2 in (1.88m) on 7

April 1876 – the leap remained a British record until 1920.

Brian Black (Blackheath and England, 10 caps 1930–3) was a member of the British four-man bobsleigh team that won the 1937 world championship. Britain retained the title the following year – their only successes in the event.

André Thieuriet (SCUF and France, five caps 1909–13) represented France in the 1908 Olympics in the 1500 metres – a distance at which he was French champion on three occasions. He failed to reach the final.

John Young (Harlequins and England, nine caps 1958–61) was the 1956 AAA 100 yards champion. He suffered from hamstring problems and was forced to withdraw from the 1956 Olympics.

Mike Cleary (New South Wales and Australia, 6 caps 1961) was credited with a time of 9.3 seconds for 100 yards in 1962, the year he represented Australia in the Commonwealth Games.

J P R Williams (London Welsh, Bridgend and Wales, 55 caps 1969–81) won the 1966 junior Wimbledon tennis singles title, beating future Davis Cup star David Lloyd in the final. Williams opted for rugby as his preferred sport.

David Whyte (Edinburgh Wanderers and Scotland, 13 caps 1965–7) leapt 23 ft 9 in (7.24 m) to become the 1959 AAA long jump champion.

J J Williams (Bridgend, Lanelli and Wales, 30 caps 1973–9) ran in the sprints for Wales in the 1970 Commonwealth Games – being eliminated in Allan Wells' heat in the 100 m and Don Quarrie's heat in the 200 m.

Gary Knight, the Manawatu and New Zealand prop forward, won a bronze medal in the wrestling tournament at the 1974 Commonwealth Games.

Guy Noves (France) and **Bruce Hunter** (New Zealand) both won their countries' national 800 metres titles.

Cecil Kershaw (England) fenced for Great Britain in three Olympic Games.

W J A Davies, the England fly-half, represented Great Britain in the sabre and foil events at the 1920 Olympics at Antwerp. Davies and Kershaw were the England half-backs on several occasions.

Ian Balding, racehorse trainer to HM The Queen and trainer of Mill Reef, the 1971 Derby winner, was captain of rugby at Marlborough and Millfield, and played full back for several seasons for Dorset and Wiltshire.

Ron Jarden, the New Zealand wing, represented New Zealand in the 1975 Admiral's Cup.

CHANGING FORTUNES

Several tourists have managed
just a few games before being
struck by injury. Indeed, the
1980 British Lions in South
Africa needed no fewer than
eight replacements. Many,
though, have been even less
fortunate, either being injured
before the tour started or in the
very first game . . .

Basie Van Wyk, the fine South
African flanker, broke a leg in
practice before the start of the
1956 tour to Australia and New
Zealand. The injury occurred in
Australia and Van Wyk never
played rugby again.

A similar accident spoilt the
1981–2 tour to Britain for the
Australian front row forward
Bruce Malouf, who broke a leg
in training at Richmond prior to
the first match.

The unwanted 'record' for the
shortest participation in a tour
match is that of **Stuart Lane**, the
Cardiff and Wales flanker, who
tore knee ligaments after 45
seconds of the first match of the
tour to South Africa in 1980
against Eastern Province.

Peter Burge, the 1908
Australian tourist to Britain,
broke his leg in the first match
of the tour, in the 24–3 win
against Devon. He missed the
rest of the tour and the chance
of an Olympic gold medal.

The stars of the 1930 British
Lions were the England half
backs **Roger Spong** and **Wilf
Sobey**, clubmates at Old
Milhillians. Sobey was injured in
the first tour match in Australia,
and didn't play again on tour.

Stan Hodgson, the Durham
City hooker, went on the 1962

British Lions tour to South Africa. In the first match of the tour he broke a leg against Rhodesia in Bulawayo and took no further part in the tour.

CFletcher of New Zealand went to Australia with the 1920 All Blacks but did not play in any of the matches. Rumour has it that Charlie Fletcher of Auckland was so popular that the rest of the tourists threatened to go on strike unless Fletcher went on tour with them!

Jock Van Niekerk, the Western Province and South Africa wing, injured his knee when attempting to stop a practice ball from falling into the sea en route to Britain for the 1931–2 tour. He injured his knee again during the opening match of the tour against the Midland Counties. He was carried off and never played rugby again at any level.

Few can have been quite so unlucky as one **Jean-Pierre Salut**, the French flanker. Picked to play against Scotland at the Colombes Stadium, Paris, on 11 January 1969, he tripped and severely injured an ankle coming up the steps onto the pitch. He took no part in the match. He was replaced before the start by a prop, Jean Iracabal of Bayonne,

who failed to enter the record books as the first substitute in international rugby to play in the whole match. France lost the match 6–3.

Dickie Lloyd of Ireland was another – like Salut – not to make the kick-off. Although photographed with the team before the game in Belfast against Wales in 1914, Lloyd, who was captaining the side, tore a muscle in the warm-up after a collision with a team-mate, and was replaced by Harry Jack. It was Ireland's last match before the First World War and Wales won 11–3.

Tom Holliday, the British Lions full back in South Africa, was injured in the first match of the 1924 tour and missed all the remaining games.

Ken Goodall, the Ireland back row forward, was flown out to join the British Lions party on their 1968 tour to South Africa. On 29 June, at Springs, the Lions beat Eastern Transvaal 37–9 in a match in which John O'Shea, the Cardiff prop, was sent off. Goodall broke his thumb in that match, his first and last match on the tour.

Peter Gerrard was selected to play for New Zealand against the British Isles in 1904. He developed a carbuncle on his knee, was forced to withdraw and was not selected again.

H E Eagles was one of the successes of the 1888 British Isles tour to Australia and New Zealand. The Swinton forward returned with hopes of a first England cap only to find that England (wooden spoonists in 1887) had declined to take part in the 1888 and 1889 championships. Harry Eagles never played for England.

Tom Stone, **Harry Edwards** and **Charles Anderson** were selected to play for Wales against Ireland on 13 March 1937. The match was postponed due to snow. When the game was eventually played on 3 April 1937, all three had been dropped, and all three were destined not to gain a Welsh cap.

Steve Smith flew out to South Africa to act as substitute scrum-half for the British Lions in the final Test match. He spent just two days in the country, and was a little unlucky not to get onto the pitch after such a journey!

WM Lowry, the Birkenhead Park wing, was photographed with the England team before the match against Wales at Swansea on 17 January 1920, yet when the teams ran onto the field he had been replaced by **H L V Day**, the Army flyer. No definite reason was given – various hints were dropped about Lowry not being suited to the sticky pitch but some suspected that it had more to do with Lowry simply having played badly the previous week. Lowry won his sole cap in England's next game; Wales won that game 19–5.

Newport's **Tom England** was selected to play for Wales against Scotland on 1 February 1890. He withdrew injured and was replaced by Jack Bancroft, who went on to represent Wales on 33 occasions over a period of 11 years. England was never capped by his country.

On 5 February 1883, Ireland played England at Whalley Range, Manchester, with 14 men for most of the game. **R W Hughes** of Northern Ireland Football Club was still suffering from sea-sickness after an appalling sea crossing the previous day, and took virtually no part in the game. The match ended in a win for England.

The sad death of the British Isles' first overseas tour captain, **R L Seddon**, has been noted elsewhere in *Rugby Shorts*, but another 1888 tourist and Yorkshireman, **J P Clowes**, was suspended and declared a professional, before he had played a single match on tour.

C E Murnin of Australia was another who suffered from the perils of the sea. He was selected for the 1908 tour to Britain but never made the English Channel; when the boat docked in Naples, he was taken off seriously ill and returned home.

Ivan Digby Bramwell was selected as replacement for the 1929 tour to Australia but was refused time off work. He was never selected for New Zealand again.

Frank Clayton was selected for the first New Zealand tour to Australia in 1884, but his bank employers didn't believe him, so he was refused permission, and was never selected again.

G P Denholm was invited on two All Black tours, to South Africa in 1976 and to France in 1977. His successful legal practice precluded time off and he was never capped.

Robert Whiteside was chosen for the 1884 New Zealanders' tour to Australia, but was then omitted from the sailing party because 'he failed to agree terms'!

It is not often that selectors are unfortunate but they appeared so in the case of **Bert Solomon**, the Redruth centre, who had a fine debut for England in the 11–6 win against Wales in the first international to be staged at Twickenham. Solomon refused all further selections to play for England, saying it was too far to travel and that he was happy just to play for Redruth.

W B Smyth travelled to the Oval to play for Ireland against England in 1875. His colleague **H B Robinson** knew the way to the Oval, but preferred to visit his family in another part of London. Both were never picked again for Ireland, Robinson deservedly; Smyth, though, was unfortunate.

Lime burns sustained on the pitch caused **Bobby Windsor**, the Welsh hooker, to miss the game with England in 1979. Markings on the Pontypool pitch a week earlier caused several players to receive treatment. Windsor did not add to his tally of 28 caps.

Unlucky or just plain daft? **Howard Marshall**, the Blackheath fly-half, played his one and only game for England against Wales on 7 January 1893 at Cardiff. Wales won 12–11 and Marshall was dropped for the next match against Ireland. The decision to drop Howard Marshall seems incredible – he scored three tries against Wales on his debut! But he was never picked again.

Christian Vereilles was selected to play for France in what proved to be his country's first ever win in international rugby. On his way to the game, he stopped at Lyon to buy a sandwich. The train left without him, and he failed to reach the ground on time. Almost inevitably, after a result like that, France were not disposed to pick M Vereilles again.

JH Mir, the Lourdes scrum-half, was selected to play his first game against Scotland on 13 January 1968. But when his Lourdes half-back partner, Jean Gachassin, was injured, Mir was removed to make way for the Camberabero brothers. However, France played badly in an 8–6 win, and Mir was brought into the team later in the year.

THE LUCKY ONES

Some of those who have benefited from the misfortunes of others have been:

Harry McCracken, the NIFC scrum-half, gained one cap for Ireland against Wales at Lansdowne Road on 13 March 1954 when he replaced John O'Meara, who ricked his back sleeping in the team hotel the night before the game.

The Guy's Hospital player **Arnold Alcock** was amazed to receive a call-up to play against South Africa in 1906. The student doctor was an average player. When he arrived at the England camp he was informed that his letter should have gone to Andrew Slocock, of the neighbouring Blackheath club. Despite the fact that England held the Springboks to 3–3, the fortunate Alcock was never picked again.

When Christian Vereilles failed to arrive in Paris after the sandwich incident (*see previous page*), **Franquenelle**, who played rugby for the local Racing Club, was called to arms. He played well in France's first ever international win, and was picked twice more.

Dr A Griffin of Edinburgh University, with a Welsh-sounding name, played his only game for Wales against Scotland at Edinburgh in 1883. It was generally thought that Griffin just made up numbers, and the good doctor never played for Wales (or Scotland) again.

Frank Purdon and **H M Jordan**, Welshmen both, made their debuts for Ireland against Wales at Cardiff in 1884. Purdon had already played four times for Wales and was never picked again, but Jordan was more fortunate and played well against his 'homeland'. Wales gave him three caps from 1885–9.

Gregory Wade, the England wing, scored three tries on his debut against Wales in 1882. But he would not have played had Philip Newton, the Blackheath forward, not got lost on the way to Swansea.

AGAINST THE ODDS

Richard Conway of New Zealand gained 13 caps as a back row forward between 1958–65. Conway suffered a septic finger during the trials for the 1960 tour to South Africa. As normal healing processes would have taken too long, Conway had his finger amputated. He played in three Tests on that tour, and a further four Tests in 1965.

Bill Redmond, the Bristol and England scrum-half, played for England twice in 1968–9. He had the sight of only one eye.

The fine South African flanker **Martin Pelser**, who won 11 caps from 1958–61, also lost the sight of one eye in an accident as a schoolboy.

That extraordinary French character, **Marcel-Frederic Lubin-Lebrere** from Toulouse, made the French team just before the First World War. He served in the war, lost an eye, and had 23 pieces of shrapnel removed from his body. He returned to the French team for a further 13 caps between 1920–5. He then became Mayor of Toulouse.

Bob Williams, the Cardiff and Wales full back, collected four caps between 1912–14. Despite the position he occupied having a requisite for safe hands, Williams managed to overcome the loss of three fingers on one hand and partial paralysis in the other.

The Racing Club flanker **Robert Thierry** won an Olympic gold medal for France in 1920, one of four caps he gained during his career. Like Redmond and Pelser, Thierry had only the sight of one eye.

Jock Wemyss was another who continued his career despite a major visual handicap. He lost an eye and was partially blinded in the other eye during the First World War, but continued to play international rugby after the war.

James Hutchinson, the 1906 England wing, had a deformity of the hand after an accident as a child in Durham with a harvesting machine.

Colin White, the Gosforth prop who won his first England cap at the age of 34 in 1983, lost three fingers in a forestry accident in 1978. He had just joined the Gosforth club.

Thomas Gordon of NIFC, who gained three caps from 1877–8, played with the handicap of having only one arm.

Danny Vietch played for British Columbia on 26 September 1959 against the British Lions. He too had only one arm.

T Gray of Northampton and Heriots FP played for Scotland in 1950–1 with a special boot – the result of having half his foot amputated after the Second World War.

EXCUSES, EXCUSES

Excuses, white lies and damned lies are part of rugby's folklore. Here are a few gentlemen whose flair for invention off the field matched their skill on the pitch . . .

John 'Dickie' Uzzell, the Newport centre, scored the winning drop goal for his club in the 3–0 win against the All Blacks on their 1963–4 tour to Britain, the only defeat that the tourists suffered. Uzzell had asked for time off studies from St Luke's College, Exeter, in order to visit his sick father, who 'recovered' enough to watch the game from the stand. Uzzell received a reprimand from the college principal – and his first cap when Wales played the All Blacks later on the tour.

John Macaulay, the Limerick and Ireland forward, had to get married in order to get time off to play in the 1887 international

against England. He had already used up his annual leave.

Charles Chapman of Cambridge University and England won his first cap against Wales in 1884 by persuading the incumbent of his position, Arthur Evanson, to retire.

Fred Alderson was voted into the England captaincy against Wales by fellow players in 1891 on two counts: first, he had travelled furthest, which impressed his team-mates; and second, his excuse for being late that he had 'run into Dick Turpin' also won their admiration. Alderson played for Hartlepool Rovers.

The NIFC and Ireland full back **D B Walkington** often used to take the afternoon off work to go to the opticians. Walkington, capped eight times between 1887 and 1891, played wearing a monocle, which he used to take off and store in his shorts every time he made a tackle.

FUNNY OLD GAME

Some of the best-kept rugby stories are secrets for obvious reasons. Others, sadly, can fall the wrong side of law and order. Here is a selection of the more humorous tales:

The 1974 Lions provided enjoyment on and off the field. Off the field the Lions were taken to the Kruger Park, South Africa's most famous National Park, for a few days' relaxation. Two planes were hired – one for players, another for provisions. The provisions (or beer) plane was dispatched 24 hours later for a refill!

A daffodil-eating contest on the same tour ended with the two finalists, Bobby Windsor (Wales) and Sean McKinney (Ireland) both having eaten their quota of daffodils. McKinney confided in an interview to the BBC's Cliff Morgan that he had been declared the winner because he had eaten a rubber plant as well.

The first recorded streaker at a rugby match, whose photograph complete with a policeman's helmet discreetly positioned adorns the Rugby Club in Hallam Street, London W1, was at Twickenham on 16 February 1974, during the England v Ireland match. The streaker was actually an Australian, William O'Brien.

Streaking then became commonplace. Thankfully, no one could compete with Erika Roe, who set standards impossible to match, and streaking eventually died. For the record, Miss Roe's performance came at half time during the match between England and Australia on 2 January 1982. Her co-streaker was Ms Sarah Bennett, who received little publicity.

When the Australians arrived in Britain for their first tour, and became known as the Wallabies rather than being named after the snake Bertie, who was their mascot, few realized that the snake was actually alive. That was until the serpent reached Wales. It died the day after the 15–0 win against Wales, and the Wallabies promptly lost their first match on the tour 8–3 to Llanelli.

Four Welshmen were asked to vacate the premises before the 1974 Wales v France match at Cardiff Arms Park for attempting to impersonate the percussion section of the St Alban Band.

Several fixtures have seen teams pass each other on the way to each other's grounds, both sides thinking theirs was the away fixture. One such journey was made by members of the Mombasa RFC and Kenya Harlequins RFC from Nairobi, who were each equally stunned to see their opponents travelling through the Tsavo National Park in the opposite direction!

Ireland arranged part of their centenary tour to New Zealand in 1975 to encompass a game against Fiji. On arrival they were told that Fiji were on a full-scale tour in Australia.

A tie salesman in Wales has for sale a souvenir tie – available to all those Welshmen who have seen Wales lose to Romania both in the home international (1988) and the away game in Bucharest (1984).

The 1963 Combined Universities (Oxford and Cambridge) hatched a plan by which the hotel manager's room was moved – to the front lawn.

A match between CASI and Hindu in Argentina was called

off just after the start when local police suspected that the match was a front for a political meeting, not a First Division match.

The France v Ireland programme in 1980 is a collector's item. It includes a spectacular misspelling of Colm Tucker, the Ireland back row, when the T of Tucker was replaced by an F!

Saintes RFC arranged a tour to Czechoslovakia to play Sparta Prague, Brno and VSS Kosice in 1974. Czech border officials refused to believe them, and refused the French team entry. They drove home. On the way, they stopped at Colmar to play the locals, and lost 87–6.

The Paris police admitted before the 1985 France v Wales match that it was their policy to 'arrest' Welshmen for a period during the Saturday of the match 'so that they could go home and tell their friends what to expect'. *Le Figaro*, 18 March 1985.

Nicknames are the vogue in rugby circles . . . some, though, can be cruel; the fine Lansdowne back and Irish international Larry Bugler was called 'Fat Cupid' and the Dublin University centre and Irish international David Rambaut was nicknamed 'the Little Fat Fellow'. Nicknames came into vogue from the 1900s

The Swedish team to play Denmark in a 1974 FIRA championship match were caught in an iceflow, and remained stuck solid for eight days.

The French aviator M D'Oisy kicked off in the France v Ireland match on New Year's Day 1925, the practice being discontinued due to his remarkable reluctance to leave the field of play.

In 1983 Dynamo Moscow visited Polytechnica Leningrad for a Soviet first division match. Dynamo won 6–0, courtesy of two penalties . . . Two months later the clubs admitted that they had agreed the score on the phone – neither club had left their respective cities.

Roan Antelope RFC have claim to the world's highest posts at 110ft 6in (33.5m) at their ground in Luanshya, Zambia. However, both Sydney RFC (Australia) and Villiers les Nancy (France) reported failed attempts to surpass the record – on both occasions the organizers had forgotten to take into account the fact that the uprights needed to be sunk 14ft (4.2m) into the ground in order to stabilize the posts.

BIZARRE INTERNATIONALS

The wettest international is considered to be the New Zealand v Scotland game on 14 June 1975. Vast areas of the ground were covered in surface water, photographers had a field day, and New Zealand won 24–0. So bad were the conditions that not one of the 13 penalties awarded resulted in a kick at goal, despite the presence of Joe Karam (NZ) and Andy Irvine (Scotland) on the field.

On 23 February 1929, the Ireland v Scotland game at Lansdowne Road was won by Scotland 16–7. Jack Arigho, the Irish centre, could not reach the posts after being awarded a try, being unable to thread his way through the encroaching crowd. Meanwhile a fine tackle by the Scottish full back Aichison on Byers, who had also crossed the try line, was disallowed because the crowd were again all over the pitch. Happily this was the last time that tries were disallowed for this reason.

The 'phantom' international took place at Bristol City FC's ground at Ashton Gate on 18 January 1908. Wales won by the then very high points score of 28–18. The match included no fewer than eight tries, but very little was seen of it, due to thick fog. Over 25 000 'witnessed' the match, with the scores telegraphed by word of mouth to the media.

South Africa's international against the USA on 28 September 1981 at Glenville, New York, was attended by 100 police and half that number of spectators. South Africa, who won 38–7, had been under threat from demonstrators, so the match took place on a secluded polo field in the early hours.

A candidate for the strangest international ever played must be the New Zealand v Australia match on 6 September 1913. The weather conditions were so bad that the game was played over four periods of 20 minutes – the only known occasion when two halves were not played. New Zealand won 30–5. At the end of each quarter hot drinks were brought out to the players, who were then allowed to change into warm, clean gear. The press were allowed to shower with the players after the game.

The final Test of the Springboks' 1981 tour to New Zealand was played at Auckland on 12 September. The match itself was a superb encounter which was won, and with it the series, by New Zealand 25–22, but it was played in conditions of great adversity; off the pitch there were numerous distractions. A bogus referee stole the ball at the start and kicked it into the crowd and the game was played to the accompaniment of some 50 low passes from a light aircraft dropping anti-apartheid leaflets and flour bombs, one of which knocked out the New Zealand prop, Gary Knight.

The Five Nations Championship drawn match between Ireland and Wales (3–3) was played at the odd time of November 1962. It had been postponed from the previous season due to the smallpox outbreak in the Rhondda Valley.

The most postponed international appears to be the game at Inverleith, Edinburgh, on 4 March 1899 between Scotland and Wales. Scotland won 21–10 at the fifth attempt to play the match, following four postponements.

THE STATE OF
THE NATIONS

Jack Van der Schyff, who missed the conversion that would have given South Africa a 24–22 win in the first Test of the 1955 series with New Zealand was dropped after that international. He received so much unwelcome publicity that he disappeared into the outback and became a crocodile hunter. So successful was his new vocation that he took it up full time.

Herman Breukhuizen, who played once against the 1896 British Lions for South Africa, later became personal chaplain to President Kruger.

One of the major selectorial blunders of all time may have been perpetrated in 1974. To counteract the British Lions forwards, South Africa selected the Free State No 8, **Gerrie Sonnekus** – height 6 ft 4 in (1.95 m) and weight 16 st 5 lb

(104 kg) to play scrum-half in the third Test at Port Elizabeth. The British Isles won 26–9. Sonnekus had never played scrum-half in his life at any level. Ten years later he won his second cap in his proper No 8 position against England, and South Africa won 33–15.

The man who was reputed to open his mouth only to eat, the 1906 Springbok tour captain to Britain, **Paul Roos**, would regularly cover vast distances to play. He used to cycle each weekend from Pietersburg, where he was a teacher, to Pretoria, a round trip of 160 miles, in order to play. Roos, a pastor in the Dutch Reformed Church, refused to contemplate anything but religion on a Sunday.

Stephen Joubert had given up all hope of donning the Springbok jersey. He retired from the game and went to Amsterdam to study medicine at

he university. During his exams
e received a letter asking him to
join the 1906 Springboks in
ritain. He left his exams, joined
he tour, and finished up playing
n all three Tests.

Aaron Okey Geffin, the
pringbok lock on their 1950-1
our to Britain, was born
without any registered Christian
ames. He gave himself the
ame Aaron, and registered his
ickname Okey.

The Springbok prop **Ben Du
Toit** was invited to join the
937 tour party to New Zealand.
He declined the invitation, but,
upon turning up to watch the
our trial, changed his mind. He
hanged, played in the second
alf, and was re-selected for the
our.

The Stellenbosch University
crum-half **Dauncey Devine**
played against the 1924 British
Lions in the third Test of the
eries. Four years later he gained
his second cap, against New
Zealand. In 1937, no fewer than
4 seasons after his first cap, he
was perilously close to being
elected for the tour to Australia
nd New Zealand.

Reserve forward **Howard Watt**
greeted the successful win by
South Africa in the second Test
against New Zealand in 1937 by
managing to suffer a hairline
fracture of the right ankle,
caused by jumping up and down
in delight in the grandstand.

In 1921 **Frank Mellish** played
for two countries in the same
year. He played in the
international championship for
England against both Ireland
and Wales, bringing his tally of
caps to six. Later that year he
emigrated to South Africa,
where the prop forward
represented that country in two
Tests against New Zealand. He
then finished his career by
playing for South Africa against
many of his old England team-
mates who were in the 1924
British Lions touring party.

Danie Craven, fine player,
captain and administrator,
rightly known as 'Mister Rugby',
holds a unique playing record,
that of playing in four different
positions in four consecutive
internationals. He began the
sequence by playing centre in
the fourth Test against Australia
at Port Elizabeth in 1933 in an
11-0 win.

For the fifth Test at
Bloemfontein he reverted to his
best position, scrum-half, in a
match won 15-4 by Australia.

South Africa's next Test was four years later – also against Australia – where he appeared as fly-half in a 9–5 win, and finally in the next Test he was selected at No 8 in a tactical move, as South Africa won 26–17 at Sydney.

The captain of the 1937 tourists to Australia and New Zealand, the Greytown farmer **Philip Nel**, was – like Paul Roos – a long-distance rugby commuter. He would get up in the small hours and travel 30 miles on horseback to Greytown, then club together with others for a 75-mile taxi ride to Pietermaritzburg, where he played for the local Collegians club. In the evening the same tedious journey in reverse would be repeated.

After the South Africans had won the series in New Zealand – the first Springbok tourists to do so – Nel announced his retirement by hurling his boots into the Indian Ocean.

The International Board player with the longest name to appear in internationals is **Willem Ferdinand van Rheede van Oudtshoorn Bergh**. Luckily he was always known as Ferdie, and was one of South Africa's stalwarts between 1931–8.

In September 1949, Rhodesia beat the New Zealand tourists

10–8. In the second match, the sides drew 3–3. Of the victorious team, no fewer than four players (five had Dantjie Viljoen not been injured) came from a tiny village just off the Salisbury (Harare)–Umtali road. The village of Inyazura provided Salty du Rand, Ryk van Schoor, Koos Brink and John Morkel to the team–farmers all. Du Rand and van Schoor later became Springboks. All that remains of the local ground are the posts, barely visible now amidst the encroaching bush.

NEW ZEALAND AND AUSTRALIA

On 3 September 1949 a strange event occurred–New Zealand lost a rugby international. Not one but two. With the 'first team' in South Africa, New Zealand arranged an international with Australia at Wellington. The visitors won 11–6. That night most of New Zealand listened on radio to the other XV being beaten 9–3 by South Africa in Durban.

It was indeed an 'All Black' year for New Zealand in 1949–they played six internationals (four against South Africa and two against Australia)–and lost the lot. It is the only calendar year in which that has happened.

ST Reid, the All Black forward, rejoiced in the Christian names Sana Torium.

In 1955 **Darling Moana** wore number 15 as full back for East Coast. His next appearance was 10 years later when he wore the number 1 shirt as a prop.

A team founded in 1985 by New Zealanders on the various oil rigs in the North Sea played under the name of Oil Blacks.

An amusing interview was given by **Peter Jones** after the 1956 international between New Zealand and South Africa to listening millions on NZBC and the crowd at Auckland. Jones said 'I hope I don't have to play in another of those matches. I'm absolutely buggered.' The interview has been rebroadcast in more liberal times.

Jack Manchester, who toured Australia with New Zealand in 1934, enjoyed the nickname 'Lugger'. This was due to the disastrous effect that

scrummaging had had on the shape of his ears.

As a method of training before the 1980 international against Australia, New Zealand coach Eric Watson decided that handling disasters had to be cured. He made the threequarters practise passing with bricks. The remedy worked – the All Bricks, as they were dubbed, won 26–10 to stifle Australian laughter.

When the British Lions played Taranaki in 1977, the home team's scrum-half **Dave Loveridge** – later to become a well-known international – was laid low with a serious knee injury. An ambulance was brought onto the field, but

became stuck in the mud. The game was held up for 18 minutes and Loveridge had recovered enough to take part in the after-match dinner.

In 1951 North Island beat South Island 14–12 at Wellington, New Zealand, yet eight tries were scored – four to each side. The North managed the one conversion that proved crucial.

When a fight broke out in the Wellington Athletic v Poneke match, the referee sent off **Arthur 'Ranji' Wilson** (Poneke) for his part in the affray. Realizing that an international was looming, Ranji's brother **Wally** offered himself to the referee as the real culprit. Ranji was recalled; his place in the New Zealand team was permanent from 1908–14, whilst Wally–whom those close to the incident knew to be innocent–was banned. Wally turned to Rugby League and represented his country at that code.

Peter Phipps was selected to play for Australia against New Zealand in 1955. He was injured before the game–his brother **James** took his place. The change was so late that many sources still, incorrectly, give Peter Phipps his one and only cap.

The two outstanding goalkickers of the 1950s, the New Zealander **Bob Scott** and the South African **Okey Geffin**, both attributed their ability to kick the ball vast distances to practising barefoot. Scott also had to overcome polio as a child.

The 1884 New Zealand tourist to Australia, **Jim O'Donnell**, stayed behind to settle in Australia for sound reasons. Shortly before the tour was due to depart, O'Donnell was arrested in his home town of Invercargill, at the tip of the South Island, and accused of owing several people money. He fled the country to join the tour and opted to remain in Australia, finishing up representing his adopted country against the British tourists in 1899.

Bob McCowan was another who courted trouble. He was a solicitor who played three times for Australia against the 1899 tourists (with O'Donnell). He was found guilty of misusing £15 000 of a trust fund which had been entrusted to him and sentenced to spend 15 years in jail. He spent most of the rest of his life roaming from bar to bar in search of employment.

The Auckland and Waikato No 8 **Hugh McLaren** collected his only cap against Australia in the 14–9 defeat in 1952. He is the only player to play senior provincial rugby in every position in the scrum during his career.

At the age of 45, the former New Zealand full back **George Nepia** became the oldest player to play in a first class match when he captained the Olympian club against Ponsonby in 1950. The Ponsonby club was also

captained by a George Nepia—
his son.

Billy Wallace, the top scorer on
the 1905 New Zealand tour to
the British Isles, scored a fine try
against Cornwall. He wore a sun
hat during the entire match.

Gilbert, who converted the try,
was also in a sun hat.

Murray Jones played once for
New Zealand—in 1973 against
England. Two years later Jones
tragically died whilst trying to

rescue his two-year-old son, who had fallen from a yacht in Auckland Harbour. He was 31 years of age.

Bill Hazlett played in all four Tests against both the 1928 Springboks and 1930 British Lions. After retiring he became a racehorse owner. From 1965–9 he won over a million dollars as leading racehorse owner in the country.

The Canterbury scrum-half **Peter Harvey** was unable to tour the British Isles with the 1905 All Blacks. He was refused permission to leave his job as a lip reader. The New Zealand Premier Seddon ruled that Harvey could not be released because he was the only qualified lip reader in the country.

Chosen to tour Australia in 1938, **John Dick** contracted measles. He was forced to withdraw and was replaced by Alan Wright. When he recovered he was presented with his fare money by his club supporters. Dick arrived in time to play three matches including the final Test.

Maurice Brownlie reached the final of the New Zealand amateur heavyweight boxing championship in 1921. He was beaten by Brian McCleary, with whom he was later to tour Britain. McCleary turned professional and was his country's heavyweight boxing champion, until beaten by Tom Heeney. The same Heeney fought Gene Tunney for the world title (*see page 70*).

WALES

On 16 December 1989, **Mike Roberts**, the former Wales and 1971 British Lions lock forward, agreed to help out his old club, the then ailing London Welsh, passing on his experience in the junior teams. He was promptly selected for the London Welsh Under-23s against their London Irish counterparts. Roberts was born on 20 February 1946 – making him 43 years old at the time of the game.

The Newport lock forward **David Waters** was chosen to replace the injured Robert Norster for the internationals against France and England in 1985 at the advanced age of 30. Both internationals were, however, postponed, and by the time they were in fact played Norster had recovered full fitness. Waters did manage to collect four caps the following season – when Norster was banned after being sent off in a club match for Cardiff.

Ernest Rowland played once for Wales in 1885, before studying for the Church. In 1886 he was struck from the books of St David's College, Lampeter, for repeated gross violation of the college rules and was never ordained into the ministry. Wales also declined to select him again.

In 1937 the Cardiff and Wales three-quarter **John Roberts**, anxious to regain his place in his club's first XV, played an entire match for Cardiff Athletic against Chepstow in stockinged feet rather than return home to collect his boots, which he had forgotten.

Selected to play for Wales in 1924 against France in Paris, **Ossie Male** was summoned by the selectors on the train to Paddington and told that as he

had contravened the WRU by-laws by playing the previous weekend for Cardiff, he would not be required for the remainder of the trip. Male was sent back when the train arrived in London. Swansea's Joe Jones was given his only cap; it took Male three years to gain his next cap.

Howard Nicholls, the Cardiff wing, was in the Welsh team that won 9–6 in Dublin in 1958. Injured during the match, Nicholls was not selected for Wales again. A few years later, an X-ray showed that Nicholls had broken his kneecap during the match.

The only time that a try has been awarded jointly in international rugby was in 1930 when both **Howie Jones** and **Harry Peacock** dived on the ball simultaneously for Wales against Ireland at Swansea. Wales won 12–7.

The only player to have played on winning teams against all three major overseas tourists to Britain is **Brian Jones**, the Newport and Wales centre. He was with Newport when they beat New Zealand in 1953 and

1957. Newport also beat Australia in 1957, and Jones was in the Barbarians team which defeated South Africa 6–0 in 1961.

The Llanelli forward **Derek Quinnell** holds the enviable record of being on a winning team against New Zealand on four occasions – for Llanelli, for the British Isles twice, and in the memorable win for the Barbarians in 1973.

Former Wales and British Lions forward **Harry Jarman** died a hero at the age of 45. He jumped in front of a runaway coal truck at Talywain in order to protect a group of children who were playing close to the track.

The Irish defiance of the New Zealand 'Haka' before the 1989 international at Dublin brought several comments, not all being complimentary. However, before the 1924 match between Wales and New Zealand, Dai Hiddlestone, the Neath flanker, led the Welsh in a 'war dance' of their own. The Welsh 'Haka' was not repeated.

Capped once against the New Zealand Army team in 1919, the **Rev Bill Havard** – later Bishop of St Asaph and St David's – is also credited with scoring the first goal for Swansea Town FC, in 1920 when they were founder members of the Third Division.

John Evans captained Wales against England in 1934. It proved to be his only international – England won 9–0. Evans was not helped by the fact that 12 others were also making their first nervous appearance in Welsh jerseys.

When at Millfield School, **Gareth Edwards** won the 1965 All England Schools 200 yards low hurdles title in a record time of 22.1 seconds – a time which remained as the record until the event was abolished. Trailing in 15 yards behind in second place was Alan Pascoe, who went on to win gold medals in the 400 metres hurdles at the 1974 European Championships and Commonwealth Games, and won a silver medal in the 4×400m relay at the Munich Olympics.

The career of **Mervyn Davies**, undisputably the world's finest

No 8 forward, was brought to a sad end during the 1976 Welsh Cup semi-final. Playing for Swansea against Pontypool, Davies, the then current Welsh captain, suffered a brain haemorrhage, which brought about immediate retirement.

Legendary stories, not all true, about the deeds on and off the field of the Pontypool and Wales scrum-half **David Bishop** gained media coverage in the 1980s. What is often forgotten, though, is that in 1979 he gained the Royal Humane Society Award for rescuing a mother and daughter from the River Taff in Cardiff. In 1981 Bishop suffered a broken neck, and was told he was not allowed to play again. In 1984 he played for Wales against Australia and in 1987 began a fruitful career in Rugby League with Hull Kingston Rovers.

Norman Biggs is the youngest player to appear in an international for Wales, at 18 years and one month. Twenty years later he died the victim of a poisoned arrow in a tribal ambush in the Nigerian outback.

Bobby Brice – a policeman – was suspended in 1904 for swearing

in Welsh during the Wales v Ireland match. A spectator translated the offensive remark and reported the contents to Scots referee Crawford Finlay. Brice was suspended for nine months.

English First Division clubs Leicester and Bristol still play with letters on the backs of their shirts, but up until 1939 Wales also followed that style. They began with the letter 'A' for the full back.

The selection policy for the 1955 British Lions tourists to South Africa followed a strange form. A deliberate policy of not selecting players over the age of 30 was introduced. Amongst those to suffer was the Welsh wing Ken Jones. The policy was somewhat justified by a 2–2 draw in a thrilling series.

In differing attitudes to those of the modern era, the Swansea and Wales half backs **Evan** and **David James** were reinstated as internationals after defecting to Rugby League. They joined the 13-man code in 1892 and were welcomed back into the fold in 1899.

Arthur Gould, the Newport and Wales centre who won 27 caps for his country, rejoiced in the nickname 'Monkey' Gould. This came about after he had shinned up a post to replace the crossbar during the 1887 Wales v England match.

Wilf Wooller, the Welsh international centre and Glamorgan County Cricket Club captain (*see page 75*), was the last player to be capped as a schoolboy. He was in the Welsh team for their historic first win at Twickenham in 1933 whilst still representing Rydal School.

Generally regarded as the roughest international in rugby history was the 1914 Ireland v Wales game at Belfast, won by Wales 11-3. The Welsh pack received fierce criticism for unsporting and overzealous play, and ill-disciplined pack

leadership. The pack became known as 'The Terrible Eight' and its leader was a clergymen, the **Reverend Alban Davies**.

B H Bridie, though picked for Wales against Scotland in 1883, was believed to have been replaced by Newport's WB Norton, because Bridie had Scottish connections. Bridie, though, insisted that he did in fact play. He was a strange character. He played for Cardiff in running shoes and a frock coat, and was described by the club as being 'a son of a parson from somewhere up in the Monmouthshire hills – we wish he would go to Newport'.

ENGLAND

Ernest Woodhead made just one appearance for England in 1880. A Dublin University student, he was a late replacement because one of the England forwards had become so sea-sick on the ferry to Dublin that he had to withdraw.

Frank Wright, the Manchester half back, gained just one cap for England, in 1881 against Scotland in Edinburgh. Wright, who had Edinburgh club connections, was drafted into the team at the last moment because Henry Taylor, who had scored three tries against Ireland, missed the train from London. Though the match was drawn, Wright was never selected for England again.

Alfred Wood, the Gloucester full back, donated one of his four caps to his employers, A V Roe Ltd, the avionics firm. This was as a mark of respect for being allowed time off to train for club and country. The cap, awarded in 1908, is still at the company works.

John Willcox gained 16 caps for England from 1962–4, and was a member of the 1962 Lions team to South Africa. His sister Sheila is still the only rider to have won the Badminton three-day event three years in succession – from 1957–9.

Edward Turner, the St George's Hospital forward, was a world record holder – for the tricycle. He is reputed to have held all world records from five to 25 miles – records which, though never officially ratified, were faster at the time (1878) than the official world cycling records for the same distances.

Richard Stafford, the Bedford prop, had a marvellous career ahead of him. Aged just 19, he had already played in all four internationals of 1912. Sadly, he contracted spinal cancer and died on 1 December, a glittering career unfulfilled.

James Shaw played twice for England in 1898. He was the father of the actor Robert Shaw, famous for his role in *Jaws*.

In 1888 England were invited to join the International Board. They declined and no internationals were played that season. However, caps were awarded to players who would have been selected . . . **Arthur Robinson**, who was called to the Bar in 1890, became the first to actually be dropped from a team which never took the field in the first place. At least Robinson eventually won a full cap. Some, like **Harry Eagles** and **Percy Robertshaw**, actually had England caps without ever playing for their country.

Geoff Roberts played three times for England in 1907–8. He was awarded the OBE and was a QC. Roberts was the chief British prosecutor at the Nuremberg War Crimes Tribunal.

tries scored in a match. In August 1936, he is reputed to have scored 17 tries against Brazil at Niteroi.

On 18 March 1922 **Herbert Price** was selected to play for England against Scotland at Twickenham–a match won by England 11–5. On the same day he was also chosen to play for England against Scotland–at hockey. Price chose rugby and is credited with the fastest try ever scored at Twickenham–against Wales the following year, scoring straight from the kick-off.

Edgar Mobbs, the Northampton and England three-quarter in whose memory the annual Mobbs Memorial match is played (*see page 22*), was a genuine rugby character–he enlisted at the start of the First World War but was refused a commission because at 32 he was considered too old. So he promptly re-enlisted as a private, and raised his own rugby-based corps known as 'D' Company of the Northamptonshire Regiment. Four hundred and twenty-seven volunteers passed through the 'Regiment'.

On 16 February 1974, **Alan Old** scored 17 of England's 21 points in their 26–21 defeat by Ireland at Twickenham. On the same day his brother Chris was playing for England in the second cricket Test match against the West Indies at Sabina Park, Kingston, Jamaica.

Prince Alexander Obolensky, the England wing who scored two memorable tries in England's 13–0 win against New Zealand in 1936, claims the 'world record' for the number of

The celebrated breaking-off of fixtures in 1884 after Scotland had disputed the validity of England's try–which eventually led to the formation of the International Board to sort out–can be partially attributed to **Richard Kindersley**. The Oxford University forward scored the try that caused all the heated debates that followed, and remained blissfully unaware of the furore he had caused.

There is a cemetery overlooking the sea at Menton, just to the east of Monte Carlo. Buried in the same row of graves are **William Webb Ellis**, **Percy Carpmael** – who founded the Barbarians – and **George Keeton**, a former England hooker. It was Keeton's burial in 1949 that confirmed the whereabouts of Ellis' grave.

One of the rarer occupations was that of **Edward Jackett**, capped 13 times from the Leicester and Falmouth clubs as full back from 1905–8. He was a nude artists' model.

Frank Isherwood gained a sole cap whilst with the Ravenscourt Park club in 1872. He spent his working life as an oil prospector in Dracula country, in the Carpathian and Transylvanian Alps in Romania.

William Holmes was England's full back throughout 1949. Born in Buenos Aires in 1928, he returned after the 1949 season to play in both Tests for Argentina against France. A month later he got married; then, tragically, within two days, had died of typhoid fever.

Philip 'Baby' Hancock (*see page 147*) was one of rugby's great commuters. He travelled from Wiveliscombe in Somerset to Blackheath to play – which meant a 26-mile cycle ride to Taunton station, a return train journey of 340 miles, and a cross-London bus ride. He often had to walk the first stage of his journey.

Joseph Green played at half-back for England in the first-ever rugby international against Scotland at Raeburn Place in 1871. He was injured in the first few minutes of the game, was carried off and never played again at any level.

Herbert Gamlin, the Wellington and England full back, capped 15 times from 1899–1904, had another sporting claim. As a county cricketer for Somerset he caught Archie MacLaren at Taunton for 424 in 1895 – MacLaren's innings being the highest score ever made in first class cricket in England. Gamlin was nicknamed 'the Octopus'.

Clive Ashby, the Wasps scrum-half, belatedly won three caps

for England in 1966–7. He was at the time still being hunted by the Mozambique army for deserting national service.

Barry Cumberlege gained eight caps for England between 1920–2. However, 10 years before his first cap, he had been selected to tour with the British Lions to South Africa. Cumberlege rejected the invitation – he was still at Durham School and his headmaster insisted he took his exams.

Similarly, the Dean of Trinity College, Oxford, refused permission for two of his students, **Edward Nash** and **Charles Crosse**, to play for England in 1875 against Scotland because of poor exam results.

George Podmore, the Oxford forward, was unable to complete the 1873 university match against Cambridge, who won. Podmore was attacked and badly bitten by a dog during the game.

Sir Lancelot Edward Barrington-Ward played for England on four occasions during the 1910 season. Between 1936–52, he became the Surgeon to His Majesty King George VI and until 1953 to Her Majesty the Queen.

IRELAND

The Irish forward **John Coffey** added another cap to his tally of 18 in strange circumstances. Having not played internationally for two seasons, he called into the Irish dressing-room before the game against France in 1910 to wish the team good luck. An Irish forward, Albert Solomons, felt so unwell that Coffey, who had enjoyed some refreshment prior to the game, was persuaded to play. The game, played on 28 March in Paris on a Monday, was won by Ireland 8–3.

Bill Cunningham, the Ireland half back, emigrated to South Africa in 1923 after winning his eighth and final cap. He set up a dentistry business in Johannesburg, and had not even trained for 18 months when he was invited to join the British Lions tour after two three-quarters had been injured on the tour. Cunningham played in the drawn third Test against South Africa in Port Elizabeth.

Twice capped by Ireland in 1912, **Bill Edwards** declined further selections. Five months later Edwards, who was a swimming champion, became the first to swim Belfast Lough; he did so to raise money for Malone clubhouse.

Sartorial elegance on the field arrived in the shape of Basil MacLear, the Ireland three-quarter. He wore white gloves throughout his career – he had 11 caps from 1905–7.

Earlier in his career he managed to talk his way into an England trial but was turned away as being not good enough.

A mystery that was never cleared up – Ireland arrived at Cardiff in 1884 to play Wales with two players short of a full complement. Wales obliged by loaning two players – H M Jordan and F J Purdon. However, many believe that it was not Purdon who played but the Newport forward John McDaniel. What makes the story even more confusing is that the team sheet listed 15 Irishmen, and failed to mention the two who did not put in an appearance.

As president of the Heinz Corporation, the Ireland and British Isles wing **Tony O'Reilly** could afford some luxury. But on his recall to the Ireland team for a late inclusion in the 1970 match against England at Twickenham, O'Reilly arrived for the squad session and match in a chauffeur-driven Rolls-Royce. When quietly rebuked by his team-mates for 'unnecessary showmanship' he explained that 'I have been doing that all season at the London Irish . . .'

C F G T Hallaran and **Vice-Admiral Sir Peverill-William Powlett** – rugby internationals both – won the equivalent of what is now the George Medal for bravery after HMS *Fiji* had been sunk off Crete in 1941.

The notion that rugby forwards are not the brightest of specimens has been dispelled by the London Irish and Ireland prop **Ollie Waldron**. His occupation is that of nuclear physicist.

SCOTLAND

Born in Nelson, New Zealand, in 1878, **Alfred Nolan** came to Edinburgh University and won seven caps for Scotland between 1901 and 1903. Selected to play against New Zealand in 1905, Nolan withdrew, citing 'loyalty to my place of birth'. He was not picked again for Scotland.

Neil McPherson, a Scottish international who played in Wales for Newport, was a victim of his country's stringent amateur code. In 1924 he was banned *sine die* by the SRU for accepting the gift of a clock from Newport RFC in recognition of their unbeaten season in 1922–3 when they won 35 and drew

four of their 39 games. The ban was later lifted, but McPherson never played for Scotland again.

Scotland's international stand-off half **Ian Robertson**, playing for the Public School Wanderers against Kodak at Harrow, lined up a drop at goal. At that moment, the posts, buffeted by high winds, were blown to the ground. Robertson paused, then dropped the ball between the fallen posts, and was correctly awarded the three points for a drop goal.

Robertson also claimed a part share in Rubstic, the Grand National winner in 1979. What is certain is that most of the horse was owned by the Scotland and British Lions No 8 forward, **John Douglas**.

The Scotland winger **Roger Baird**, who won 27 caps between 1981 and 1988, has the unenviable record of failing to score a try in any of those internationals, believed to be a record for a wing. However, he did manage to score a try for the

British Isles in the third Test against New Zealand in 1983.

Jim Calder was recalled to the Scotland team for the match against France in 1986. When he withdrew injured, he was replaced by his twin brother **Finlay**, who later went on to captain the successful 1989 British Lions in Australia.

John Allan, the burly Melrose, Barbarians and Scotland prop, enjoyed a more delicate line of occupation. He was a nurse at the local hospital.

Scotland deprived the 1924–5 New Zealand 'invincibles' of the Grand Slam. The tourists had beaten the other three home nations, and would beat France, but Scotland declined to play. The reason was that they had 'outgrown their Inverleith ground'.

The most capped of the nobility is Lord Bannerman. Known as **J M Bannerman** of Oxford University, Glasgow HSFP and Scotland, he played in 37 internationals between 1921–9.

FRANCE

Jacques Fouroux, the French coach, has been accused in the 1980s of some weird decisions both on and off the field. As a player, though, he was the victim of similar indecision on the 1975 tour to South Africa. Fouroux and **Richard Astre** were appointed joint captains, which was understandable, but both were scrum-halves. The tour was chaos from a tactical point of view.

Capped five times on the wing by France between 1963–8, **Pierre Besson** was not the fastest in the family. That honour fell to sister Collette, who won the 400 metres gold medal at the 1968 Olympics, beating Lillian Board in a dramatic finish.

Another for the strange occupations department – **Jean Barthe**, from the Lourdes club, who won 26 caps, owned a bazaar and a pilgrimage souvenir shop.

A job that most would like –
René Bienes was a utility
forward good enough to win 29
caps from 1950–6. He played for
Cognac, the brandy centre of
the world, and had a job tasting
the product.

France's highest award, the
Legion d'Honneur, was

bestowed upon the international
forward **Maurice Boyau**.

Two Prime Ministers of the
future met in an international
between France and Romania in
1937. **Jacques Chaban Delmas**,
Prime Minister of France
between 1969–72, was in the
French team, while **Ion Papa**
went on to become Prime
Minister of Romania.

In a 1974 match between Villiers les Nancy and Villeneuve in the Lorraine League, Villeneuve winger **Guy Thomas** was upended by a snowman, erected by Villiers full back **Rouyer** – built out of boredom and cold by Rouyer, whose team were 65–3 ahead at the time.

The French second row partnership (1945–9) of **Robert Soro** of Lourdes (21 caps) and **Alban Moga** of Begles (21 caps) were universally nicknamed at the time 'Ham and Eggs'. Which one was which was never clear.

In 1976–7 France won the International Championship with the same 15 players and did not concede a try. The team was: Aquirre; Harize, Sangali, Bertranne, Averous; Romeu, Fouroux (captain); Paparemborde, Paco, Cholley; Imbernon, Palmie; Skrela, Rives, Bastiat.

Conversely, the worst record in international rugby would be that of **Aime Cassayet** of Narbonne and France. He was capped on 26 occasions in the International Championship and was on the losing side 22 times.

He was in the Olympic finals of 1920 (which France may have lost – see *Olympic Rugby*) and 1924 (which they certainly lost).

He also led France to a 30–6 defeat by the 1925 New Zealand XV. A fine player in a thoroughly bad side, he tragically died of cancer at the age of 28 in May 1927.

Two established French internationals, the half-backs **Didier Camberabero** and **Henri Sanz**, were banned from playing an international in the FIRA championship in 1984 against Poland. Both were at the time completing their national service, and as such were thought to be a security risk.

In 1984 the FFR decreed that, because the national team were due to leave that evening for New Zealand, their championship final between Beziers and Agen would have to be decided on a shoot-out if the scores were level at full time. Sure enough, the clubs were level at 15–15 at the final whistle – the final was then decided by penalties taken in turn from the 22. Beziers won the soccer-style shoot-out 3–1, but the experiment has yet to be repeated.

Vergt is a small French town situated just north of the Dordogne Valley. In November 1984, Vergt and Capiteux played a violent match in Group 9 of the Third Division. Four players were sent off, but Vergt felt that they were treated too harshly by the disciplinary committee of the French Rugby Union (FFR).

So they decided to protest against the bans on players and the fines imposed, and in their next league game, against Lermont, Vergt fielded 11 players only, the minimum necessary for the match not to be called off.

After ten minutes the referee called the game off as the Vergt players stood around like dummies whilst Lermont waltzed round the statuesque opposition to build a 42–0 lead.

The following week, the same 11 players turned up for the match against Gujan-Mestres. Adopting exactly the same tactics, Vergt lost 236–0 on 11 November 1984 to Gujan-Mestres.

A week later on 18 November, the difficulties still not resolved with the FFR, Vergt met Lavardac with 14 players, one of whom had served his suspension. This time the 'dummies' surpassed themselves. Their static opposition allowed Lavardac to rattle up a score of 360–0, a score made up of 66 tries, 40 conversions and two drop goals. A world record, surely?

FROM UNION TO LEAGUE

Since the breakaway of the Northern Union in 1895 more than 200 Rugby Union Internationals from the four home countries have switched codes. Forty-one of them went on to become dual Internationals.

The most capped Rugby Union international to switch codes is Steve Fenwick who played for Wales on 30 occasions and the Lions four times before switching to Rugby League with Cardiff City in 1981. Other players with 20 caps or more who made the switch to the professional game have been:

Jonathan Davies (Wales) 27 caps, who joined Widnes in 1988–9
Terry Holmes (Wales) 25 caps + 1 Lions, who joined Bradford Northern in 1985–6
Rob Ackerman (Wales) 22 caps + 2 Lions, who joined Whitehaven in 1985–6
David Watkins (Wales) 21 caps + 6 Lions, who joined Salford in 1967–8
William Welsh (Scotland) 21 caps + 1 Lions, who joined London Highfield in 1933–4
Paul Moriarty (Wales) 21 caps, who joined Widnes in 1988–9
John Devereux (Wales) 21 caps, who joined Widnes in 1989–90
James Webb (Wales) 20 caps + 3 Lions, who joined St. Helens in 1912–13

Six men have been dual tourists with the British Lions and the Great Britain Rugby League team. All were Welsh backs:

	RU Tour (Club)	RL Tour (Club)
Jack Morley	1930 (Newport)	1936 (Wigan)
Lewis Jones	1950 (Llanelli)	1954 (Leeds)
Terry Price	1966 (Llanelli)	1970 (Bradford N)
Maurice Richards	1968 (Cardiff)	1974 (Salford)
David Watkins	1966 (Newport)	1974 (Salford)
John Bevan	1971 (Cardiff Coll)	1974 (Warrington)

The following Rugby Union International captains went on to play the professional game:
Wales David Watkins, Steve Fenwick, Terry Holmes, Jonathan Davies
England Richard Lockwood
Ireland Robin Thompson (Thompson also skippered the British Lions)

Leeds have recruited a record 30 Rugby Union internationals, while Oldham have recruited the most former England internationals – nine.

Cardiff have lost the most ex-internationals to the professional game: 24; Llanelli are next with 22 departures.

Robert Lloyd (Pontypool-Halifax) is the only scrum-half to have been a dual international.

In 1988–9 Jonathan Davies became the most expensive player to switch codes when he joined Widnes for a £225,000 contract.

The first player to switch codes for a 'sizeable' fee was Daniel Rees, the Swansea centre who signed for Hull KR in 1905. He received the sum of £300.

David Watkins was the first ex-Rugby Union International to command a five-figure fee when he joined Salford from Llanelli for £15,000 in 1967–8.

The following six are the only present-day clubs never to have signed a Rugby Union International:

Chorley Borough; Bramley; Carlisle; Doncaster; Featherstone Rovers; Nottingham City.

The full list of 46 dual internationals (at 31.5.90) is:

Player	Country	RU Club	1st RL Club	Season turned Professional
Arthur Bassett	Wales	Cardiff	Halifax	1938–39
*John Bevan	Wales	Cardiff	Warrington	1973–74
David Bishop	Wales	Pontypool	Hull KR	1988–89
Francis Boylen	England	Hartlepool R	Hull	1908–09
Jim Brough	England	Silloth	Leeds	1925–26
Percy Coldrick	Wales	Newport	Wigan	1912–13
*Mike Coulman	England	Moseley	Salford	1968–69
Tom Danby	England	Harlequins	Salford	1949–50
Avon Davies	Wales	Aberavon	Leeds	1912–13
Bill Davies	Wales	Swansea	Bradford N	1939–40
Jonathan Davies	Wales	Neath/Llanelli	Widnes	1988–89
Frank Evans	Wales	Llanelli	Swinton	1921–22
Stuart Evans	Wales	Neath	St. Helens	1986–87
Keith Fielding	England	Moseley	Salford	1973–74
Ray French	England	St. Helens	St. Helens	1961–62
Jack Gore	Wales	Blaina	Salford	1924–25
Ben Gronow	Wales	Bridgend	Huddersfield	1910–11
David Holland	England	Devonport S	Oldham	1913–14
David Jenkins	Wales	Treorchy	Hunslet	1926–27
David Jones	Wales	Treherbert	Merthyr Tydfil	1907–08
*Keri Jones	Wales	Cardiff	Wigan	1968–69
*Lewis Jones	Wales	Llanelli	Leeds	1952–53
*Roy Kinnear	Scotland	Heriots FP	Wigan	1926–27
Robert Lloyd	Wales	Pontypool	Halifax	1914–15
John Mantle	Wales	Newport	St. Helens	1964–65
Roy Matthias	Wales	Llanelli	St. Helens	1972–73
Edgar Morgan	Wales	Llanelli	Hull	1921–22
*Jack Morley	Wales	Newport	Wigan	1932–33
*Malcolm Price	Wales	Pontypool	Oldham	1961–62
*Terry Price	Wales	Llanelli	Bradford N	1967–68
Glyn Prosser	Wales	Neath	Huddersfield	1935–36
Tom Rees	Wales	London Welsh	Oldham	1928–29
*Maurice Richards	Wales	Cardiff	Salford	1969–70
Johnny Ring	Wales	Aberavon	Wigan	1922–23
*Bev Risman	England	Loughborough	Leigh	1960–61
David Rose	Scotland	Jedforest	Huddersfield	1953–54
Glyn Shaw	Wales	Neath	Widnes	1977–78
Alan Tait	Scotland	Kelso	Widnes	1988–89
Joe Thompson	Wales	Cross Keys	Leeds	1922–23
David Valentine	Scotland	Hawick	Huddersfield	1947–48
John Warlow	Wales	Llanelli	St. Helens	1963–64
*David Watkins	Wales	Newport	Salford	1967–68
William Williams	Wales	Crumlin	Salford	1927–28
Peter Williams	England	Orrell	Salford	1987–88
Alf Wood	England	Gloucester	Oldham	1908–09
Tom Woods	England	Bridgwater A.	Rochdale H.	1909–10

* Indicates British Lions tourist.

In addition to those asterisked above, the following British Lions tourists also turned to the professional game:

Player	Country	RU Club	1st RL Club	Season turned Professional
Rob Ackerman	Wales	Cardiff	Whitehaven	1985–86
Ron Cowan	Scotland	Selkirk	Leeds	1962–63
Tommy David	Wales	Pontypridd	Cardiff City	1981–82
John Devereux	Wales	Bridgend	Widnes	1989–90
Keith Fairbrother	England	Coventry	Leigh	1974–75
Steve Fenwick	Wales	Bridgend	Cardiff City	1981–82
Ken Goodall	Ireland	Derry	Workington T	1970–71
Don Hayward	Wales	Newbridge	Wigan	1954–55
Thomas Holliday	England	Aspatria	Oldham	1926–27
Terry Holmes	Wales	Cardiff	Bradford N	1985–86
Ray Hopkins	Wales	Maesteg	Swinton	1972–73
Edward Jackett	England	Leicester	Dewsbury	1911–12
Keith Jarrett	Wales	Newport	Barrow	1969–70
Fred Jowett	Wales	Swansea	Hull KR	1905–06
Pat Quinn	England	New Brighton	Leeds	1956–57
Russell Robins	Wales	Pontypridd	Leeds	1958–59
Robin Thompson	Ireland	Instonians	Warrington	1956–57
James Webb	Wales	Abertillery	St–Helens	1912–13
William Welsh	Scotland	Hawick	London H	1933–34
Bryan West	England	Northampton	Wakefield T	1970–71
Brynmor Williams	Wales	Swansea	Cardiff City	1982–83
David Young	Wales	Cardiff	Leeds	1989–90

The author would like to thank those who contributed to the following books, which have helped to authenticate many statistics and stories:

Who's Who of International Rugby
Encyclopedia of New Zealand Rugby
Rugby Writers Annual (South Africa)
History of Welsh International Rugby
History of the RFU
Report on Rugby
L'Equipe Rugby